KEYWORDS | Truth

THE KEYWORDS SERIES

Identity

Truth

Gender

Experience

KEYWORDS | Truth

Other Press • New York

Copyright © 2004 Alliance of Independent Publishers, France

First published in China by Shanghai Literature and Art Publishing House
First published in France by Éditions La Découverte
First published in India by Sage India
First published in Morocco and Lebanon by Arab Cultural Center of Casablanca/Beirut
First published in South Africa by Double Storey Books
First published in the United States by Other Press, New York

Production Editor: Robert D. Hack
Text design: Kaoru Tamura and Natalya Balnova

This book was set in Joanna MT by Alpha Graphics of Pittsfield, NH.

10 9 8 7 6 5 4 3 2 1

All rights reserved. No part of this publication may be reproduced or transmitted in any form or by any means, electronic or mechanical, including photocopying, recording, or by any information storage and retrieval system, without written permission from Other Press LLC, except in the case of brief quotations in reviews for inclusion in a magazine, newspaper, or broadcast. Printed in the United States of America on acid-free paper. For information write to Other Press LLC, 307 Seventh Avenue, Suite 1807, New York, NY 10001. Or visit our Web site: www.otherpress.com.

Library of Congress Cataloging-in-Publication Data

Keywords : truth / Deborah Posel . . . [et al.].
    p. cm.
   Includes bibliographical references.
   ISBN 1-59051-106-9 (pbk. : alk. paper)
   1. Truth. I. Posel, Deborah.
 BD171.K46 2004
 121–dc22

2004006507

CONTENTS

SERIES PREFACE	vii
from *Africa* TRUTH? THE VIEW FROM SOUTH AFRICA'S TRUTH AND RECONCILIATION COMMISSION Deborah Posel	1
from *America* AMERICAN THOUGHT ABOUT TRUTH Douglas Patterson	27
from the *Arab World* ASSENT AND TRUTH IN THE MEDIEVAL ARABIC PHILOSOPHICAL TRADITION Ali Benmakhalouf	53
from *China* ON ZHEN Yang Guo-rong	85
from *Europe* TRUTH IN FRANCE Bertrand Ogilvie	101
from *India* TRUTH IN INDIAN TRADITIONS Ganesh Devy	131
ABOUT THE AUTHORS	159

SERIES PREFACE

Established on the initiative of the Charles Leopold Mayer Foundation, the KEYWORDS collection was born of a propitious encounter between a Chinese, an American, and a French publisher. The project is now being executed by the Alliance of Independent Publishers[1] that, besides its founders—Shanghai Cultural Publishers and La Découverte in France—includes Double Storey Books in South Africa, Le Centre Cultural Arabe in Casablanca and Beirut, Other Press in the United States, and Sage Publications India. The project offers fundamental notions from different cultural points of view, taking a hard look at a common object with a view from afar. The collection thereby aims to produce an intercultural dialogue and an exploration of globalization with, as point of departure, local points of

---

1. See www.fph.ch and www.alliance-editeurs.org

view on essential themes such as *experience*, *gender* (or masculine-feminine), *identity*, *nature*, and *truth*. Thus, in their respective languages, the publishers will provide the same small book on one of the words chosen beforehand, and each will then consist of six articles of about twenty pages each. For example, the notion of *truth* will, in turn, be tackled by an African, an American, an Arab, a Chinese, and an Indian writer, each of whose texts will then be translated into four languages respectively: English, Arabic, Chinese, and French. The texts will be exchanged between the publishers to come out under a same title within the same year in each of the countries in question. In short: one word and six points of view to create, if not a world, at least a book.

Such a new and difficult project had to proclaim its experimental character with all that this implies as source but also as experimentation and approximation. Furthermore, it needed a pragmatic framework and a few guiding, though equally flexible, principles. Then there was the choice of words. For some of these, we were concerned with current events, taking into account major political considerations, examinations divided along the line of contemporary debate in the terms and contexts of expression that are frequently misunderstood. The questions of *identity* and *gender* became imperative: these past few decades they have heavily mobilized public opinion and the academy. They are keywords that now circulate almost everywhere and deserve to be torn from the untrammeled use they so often get. They have gained from being set free from the ambiguities and globalizations that render them meaningless.

Obviously, the glitter of the topical is better understood when supported by a few historical and semantic reference points. By backing this up with symbolic patterns and antecedents, one can better define the outlines and what is at stake, check off implicit comparisons and their imaginary hierarchical organizations, and get rid of old references that add up like hastily assembled arrangements. Thus, the false familiarities and simultaneities, spun by the media networks, are seen more clearly. In this plural space that has no center, in which the suggestions may intersect or be ignored or excluded, the confrontation can only hold surprises. The map of problems, their formulation, the development of ideas, the range of preoccupations, the levels of historicity and abstraction, and the degree of intensity necessarily fluctuate. Hybridizations are not always recognized and identity fixations are not always where one expects to find them. Gaps of temporality run through the various societies themselves (and not just across borders) by crystallizing other forms of discontinuity. The unspoken is at least as significant as what is presented.

The complexity of the transmissions can never be sufficiently assessed; therefore, the translations pose an immediate problem. The concept of *gender*, which has nurtured entire departments in the English-speaking universities and has henceforth been adopted by international organizations, has always been the object of controversy. It is of concern today in the United States where it was born and spread, although not without polemics in the feminist camp itself, because of the problematics of transgender and queer. The Arab author will clasp it to do a libertarian rereading of the past and brilliantly serve the cause of women and homosexuals. As for the famous question of *identity*, which in its various modalities does not stop troubling politicians today, it has exciting extensions depending on whether it is reopened to a very refined question on colonialism (Africa) or refers to a game of mirrors and paradoxical deconstruction that ends up as a transcultural demand (China); whether it lends itself to a wholesome de-dramatization (on the side of the Arabs) and a swinging back of the pendulum in the United States as a reaction to earlier multiculturalism; or whether it is simply the opportunity provided here to clearly expose the terms and turns of the debate (in India and Europe).

Other concepts, if not more classical and timeless, ask to be presented when they structure worlds, that is to say when they are articulated orders but also, for many people today, a haven on the horizon of a daily life in flux. Above all, when they turn out not to be any less problematic than the first ones: What is *nature* today? How did the Arab philosophers rethink the *physis* of Aristotle or the neo-Platonists and what advantage did the theologians take of this to fight them? How does *experience* issue forth from event in China and in what way is it inexpressable? Is it still pertinent to oppose scientific *experience*, the experience lived in psychoanalytic treatment, with what Kant calls the "judgment of experience"? Why has this term acquired such imaginary bulk in the portrayal that America has of itself? By what alternate routes have we moved from one model of mathematical *truth* and universal forms of what is *true* to a pluralization, indeed its disappearance as thematic in the order of the techno-sciences? How do we report in just a few pages on *truth* according to the Vedas, the Upanishads, the great epics, Shankara, the poetic theory of Bharata, the mystic songs of the *Bhakta*, and the Gandhian ideal? The history of ideas is not an insignificant exercise, especially in a limited space and for the benefit of the other who is presumed to be ignorant—or almost ignorant—of the background. Obviously, there will only be a few lines of demarcation here allowing for the decoding of a cultural landscape or of daily life, roughly outlining the genealogy of a philosophical question, and here and there letting the game of theoretic uncoupling or loans be guessed at.

It may happen that an author decides to ignore the historical side of a concept in order to focus on a reality that stands out: How and within what boundaries did the South African Truth and Reconciliation Commission operate? Generally, however, the issues have been put in perspective by being directed at an audience abroad and also by letting everyone hear the novelty of his or her own voice in hitherto unpublished combinations. In the absence or well nigh absence of a preliminary designation (methodological, epistemological, political, and so forth) the space that becomes visible is not without relief or accidents. Some articles may well seem too "technical," others not sufficiently so. From one region to another, they differ in their levels of analysis and more generally in their disciplinary approaches: the Chinese and the Arabs pay special attention to language; Indians like to think of themselves as sociologists or anthropologists; the plural disciplines of the American *cultural studies* differ from those of the French philosophers. These texts, which are neither encyclopedic articles nor free essays, have the value of being documents: they do not aspire to being strictly representative (of a state of knowledge, a discipline, an identity) and no institution mandated them, smoothed them out, or standardized them. Speaking for themselves, they call more than anything else for being discussed, studied, and augmented. It is left up to the readers to pursue the thinking, to immerse themselves in the different points of view to try to compare and flush out the dissimilarities or the common values. We are here concerned merely with providing some insights, with preparing an encounter, and opening a space to make contact.

The choice of authors was also the object of a few minimal guidelines. Priority was given to authors—philosophers, linguists, sociologists, anthropologists, and so on—from the South of the various cultural regions concerned rather than to those who live in the West. In this first series we did not always manage it, but for the most part this will be the case. Moreover, we have attempted to act in such a way as to avoid two stumbling blocks, each of which would misrepresent the project and both of which are well known since they feed the debate on globalization today. On the one hand, we had to avoid specific characteristics that were too great, whether it concerned terminology that was too specialized, subjective idiosyncrasies, or closed attitudes expressing a denial of the other. Although it is true that we do not all support certain political positions that are expressed here and there, on the whole we fulfilled this condition. On the other hand, we were not to give in to the standardization resulting from certain contemporary infatuations: identity withdrawal or mimetic reencoding in conformity with forms of a too-marked postmodern rhetoric. The collection rests on processes of scholarly circulation, the growing internationalization of research that solicited and stimulated it. It has updated a third more or less compact space corresponding to themes and regions that divert or complicate the dichotomies between dominators and dominated. Without this implicit theoretical horizon, the complex game of appropriations, occasional restrictions, and gaps that one sees emerge from one article to another, would not have been possible.

The achievement of these small books owes a great deal to the loyal support from and help of Etienne Galliand, to whom herewith our gratitude. We also wish to express our sincere thanks to Jean Copans, Françoise Cremel, Ghislaine Glasson Deschaumes, Thomas Keenan, Michèle Ignazzi, Michel Izard, Farouk Mardam-Bey, Ramona Naddaff, Jean-Luc Racine, and Roshi Rashed.

Nadia Tazi
Paris, November 2003

Translated by Marjolijn de Jager

from *Africa*

TRUTH? THE VIEW FROM SOUTH AFRICA'S TRUTH AND RECONCILIATION COMMISSION[1]

Deborah Posel

---

1. Parts of this chapter draw on the introductory chapter to the book that I coedited with Graeme Simpson, *Commissioning the Past: Understanding South Africa's Truth and Reconciliation Commission* (Wits University Press, 2002), as well as my own chapter in this collection, "The TRC Report: What Kind of History? What Kind of Truth?" My thinking has been informed by many fascinating conversations with Graeme during our collaboration on the introductory chapter.

IN THE ERA OF late modernity (the latter half of the twentieth century and into the twenty-first), the idea of truth has become the site of an intriguing and distinctive paradox. From a philosophical point of view, the credibility of truth has been seriously destabilized.[2] The idea of an objective, reliable truth has come increasingly under fire from a range of relativist arguments insisting that truth-finding is an active, interpretative activity that is inevitably and irrevocably imprinted with the subjectivity of those who set off in its pursuit. From this standpoint, there is no detached vantage point from which to discover or adjudicate a single, absolute, and robust truth.

Versions of the relativist case span a spectrum from strong to weak. Strong relativist arguments dismiss truth altogether as a

---

2. Relativist theories of truth have a much longer history, of course. For the purposes of this chapter, it's only the more contemporary expression of this position that pertains to the argument being made here.

meaningless concept and a futile pursuit. At the other end, reluctant to forgo the notion of truth altogether, weaker relativist arguments propose more modest claims to truth with a small "t," which are subject to reasonably robust tests of evidence but strictly within the limits of a particular paradigm or way of thinking.[3]

As these academic debates have infiltrated more wide-ranging spheres of debate and analysis, popular uncertainty and skepticism about truth has grown, too. As Felipe Fernandez-Armesto (1998) writes in his popular book, *Truth: A History and Guide for the Perplexed*, "Trapped between fundamentalists, who believe they have found truth, and relativists, who refuse to pin it down, the bewildered majority in between continues to hope there is a truth worth looking for, without knowing how to go about it or how to answer the voices from either extreme" (p. 3).

From a political point of view, however, late modernity has seen a *reassertion* of the social value of truth, coupled with a renewed confidence in the prospect and importance of establishing reliably objective and authoritative benchmarks of truth. Nowhere is this conviction more insistent than in the recent global enthusiasm for the idea of truth commissions, as the vehicles of what has become known as "transitional justice."

There is no single uniform model for a truth commission; different political and historical circumstances have shaped particular truth commissions in distinctive ways. But there are defining features of all such enterprises. All truth commissions, which are constituted for a limited period of time, are invested with some sort of official authority, to produce a reliably and objectively truthful account of human rights violations over a designated period in the past (Hayner 1994). This means, too,

---

3. For a fuller account of such controversies, see, e.g., Kirkham (1992), Horwich (1990), Blackburn and Simmons (1999), and Rosenau, (1992).

that there are fundamental aspirations and epistemological conditions that all truth commissions share.

Truth commissions not only assume that the pursuit of impartial, objective truth is *possible*, they also deem it to be fundamentally *desirable*. Truth commissions are predicated on the argument that truth is good—if not essential—for the prospects of democracy in previously authoritarian, violent regimes. With the overthrow of the oppressor, responsible for all manner of moral and political harms in the past, the fate of a fledgling democracy born of violent and bloody conflict is uncertain and vulnerable. Truth commissions have inspired faith in many as a powerful means of confronting the demons of the past and unflinchingly unveiling its secrets. With this newfound openness to moral culpability in the past, it is argued, the political commitment to a new democratic and just dispensation is strengthened, in ways that help to forge a newfound sense of national unity and reconciliation. From this standpoint, therefore, not only is the idea of truth newly ascendant, expectations of what it can deliver are also optimistically high. Truth becomes the vector of a moral consensus on the wrongs of the past; the reconciliation effected in the name of these disclosures becomes the glue for a socially unified and morally robust future. Hence the paradox: philosophically, skepticism about truth has perhaps never been greater, yet this is exactly the moment at which the idea of the truth commission has gripped the political imagination.

In Africa, too, the resurgent hope of transcending histories of intense brutality and violence, and restoring democratic rule, has generated growing pockets of faith in the power of the truth commission. To date, truth commissions have been held in Chad (1992), Nigeria (1999), Uganda (1994), as well as in South Africa (begun in 1996 and yet to deliver its final report). Currently a truth commission has been agreed to in Sierra Leone, and the prospect of a truth commission in Congo has been mooted.

For truth commission enthusiasts, South Africa's Truth and Reconciliation Commission (TRC), appointed to expose and adjudicate the gross violation of human rights during much of the apartheid era, was the outstanding exemplar of the power of truth as the handmaiden of democracy. This chapter therefore focuses on the modalities of truth-production in the TRC, but seen against the backdrop of a more wide-ranging commentary on the genre of the truth commission itself.

The truth commission is a phenomenon of the late twentieth century. Since 1983 (with the inauguration of the Argentinian National Commission on the Disappeared), there have been 22 truth commissions (Hayner 2001), with at least a further six currently under discussion. Its raison d'être, along with the manner of truth expected of a truth commission, is profoundly shaped by the historical context in which the idea of a truth commission has taken hold. In a recent lecture, Charles Taylor (2002) engaged with this history by way of a discussion of the mounting preoccupation, particularly in modern democratic societies, with what he terms "negative commemoration," as distinct from "positive commemoration." Positive commemoration refers to long-standing and familiar traditions of remembering and acknowledging major acts of moral courage, valor, heroism, and leadership. By contrast, negative commemoration refers to the need to expose and confront harmful or otherwise destructive episodes in a nation's history, in the attempt to set the record straight and remedy moral or political harms done. Negative commemoration requires truth-telling, for an essentially moral purpose.

Taylor argues that in late modern societies, the effort to be democratic increasingly necessitates exercises in negative commemoration, for two reasons. First, one of the consequences of globalization has been the production of new modes of global vigilance: what happens in one part of the world is watched by, and seen to matter in, other parts of the world. This is partly a function of new technologies of transmitting and receiving information, but it is also shaped by discourses of human rights and international law, in relation to which there can be no morally disinterested position on the violation of human rights in any part of the world. Second, with the advent of discourses of multiculturalism, political and ethnic majorities in democratic societies can no longer be seen to ignore the existence and entitlements of minorities. Multiculturalism entails a recognition of diversity and a tolerance of its effects, in producing different cultures, values, and perspectives on experience. In the light of this principle of tolerance, any exclusion or marginalization of a minority becomes morally indefensible, nationally as much as internationally. The politics of democratic inclusion, therefore, requires opportunities to undo—by acknowledging—histories of marginality or oppression in ways that give voice to those previously silenced.

In short, therefore, negative commemoration has become an integral part of the moral politics of democratic nations in a global milieu. And the audiences addressed by these practices of commemoration are international as well as national.

Taylor was speaking primarily about stable modern democracies, but the advent of the notion of "transitional justice" renders his argument equally interesting in respect to developing countries in the throes of often fragile and contested transitions from authoritarian to democratic rule. A discussion of the conditions of transitional justice has become perhaps the dominant global prism on, and interest in, the prospect of democratization in erstwhile authoritarian countries. In these debates, the device of a truth commission is upheld as a fruitful means of stabilizing the fledgling democratic project. A truth commission, it is claimed, can allow for the unflinching pursuit of the truth about the past, which is as much a moral reading of prior harms done as it is the exposure of previously hidden or distorted histories of violation. From this perspective, then, the device of a truth commission fits Taylor's bill for negative commemoration extremely well, as much in respect to its propensities for unveiling a traumatic past as in the potential to rehabilitate the voices of those previously excluded from public memory. And as is the case with all instances of negative commemoration, the audiences addressed by a truth commission's efforts to rehabilitate and stabilize the democratic project are international as well as national.

If negative commemoration is the primary animating impulse of a truth commission, the production of truth by this means is fashioned by the epistemological and moral imperatives of the commemorative task. In order for a truth commission to perform its political function, it needs to be seen to deliver a particular kind of knowledge about the past: knowledge that is demonstrably impartial, objective, and authoritative. The legitimacy of the commission depends fundamentally on the perception of its findings as having been wholly untainted by any political bias, and uncontaminated by the conflicts of viewpoints that encumbered efforts to retrieve a truthful version of history under the previous authoritarian regime.

Public trust in the veracity of the "truth" produced by a truth commission also requires a perception that the practitioners of that truth are suitably equipped for the task, with expertise appropriate to the modes of historical investigation for which they were appointed—expertise that would typically involve a particular combination of research or investigative skills, and a knowledge of the relevant issues with respect to human rights. The quest for truth must be perceived to be safe in the hands of an official commission of experts who are neutral and elevated above the grubby world of local politics. From an epistemological standpoint, therefore, the very idea of a truth commission reiterates familiarly modernist assumptions about the prospects for and conditions of a reliably objective, expertly assembled, and politically disinterested body of truth.

At the same time, particularly in the case of those truth commissions that originate in an effort to effect reconciliation and/or compromise between previously hostile factions, truth commissions must also demonstrate their even-handedness and a consistent tolerance of divergent viewpoints in airing all sides of a particular story. The truth of a truth commission must acknowledge diverse subjectivities—and therefore contending versions of events—as part of the imperative to vindicate the voices of those previously excluded from official narratives of the past. But having done so, truth commissions then have to move beyond this multiplicity of versions. At the end of the day, the impulse of a truth commission is to adjudicate between different versions, to produce a single overarching narrative that is authorized as objective, expert, and morally and ideologically neutral.

The truth of most truth commissions,[4] therefore, is immediately subject to an inherent tension, born of having to authenticate—and yet adjudicate between—competing subjective perspectives, memories, and judgments on a much contested, traumatically violent, historical process. Failure to resolve this tension—and thereby capitulate to the uncertainties of multiple versions of a contentious past—would fundamentally detract from the legitimacy of the enterprise. Indeed, the prospect of an official truth commission steeped in relativist acceptances that truth is inevitably and irredeemably perspectival and subjective

---

4. The only kind of truth commission that would escape this tension would be that which sought simply to emulate the process of positivist historical research in assembling the facts, spared the political imperative of giving public voice to contending perspectives on the past.

would surely be a contradiction in terms. Putting this differently: truth commissions have to refute, rather than embrace, the paradox of their genealogy, by rebutting the philosophical skepticism about truth that has marked the late modern moment.

In the case of the South African TRC, this tension was compounded by a uniquely ambitious mandate, which proliferated an even more demanding set of expectations of the manner of truth it set out to deliver. For this reason, the TRC demonstrates, perhaps more vividly and effectively than any other commission, the complexities that attach to the official commissioning of the truth.

In 1994, South Africans witnessed the statutory eradication of the apartheid system that had prevailed since 1948, and its replacement with a commitment to constitutional democracy and a doctrine of human rights. This transition was enabled by a skillfully negotiated compromise between the outgoing exponents of minority rule, and the incoming champions of a new democratic order. In this process, the TRC was envisaged as playing a critical role in helping to fashion a new, unified, South African nation. Indeed, the proponents of the TRC had extremely high hopes for its powers of reconciliation wrought through truth.

This meant, in turn, that the production of historical truth had to serve multiple purposes. In the first instance, the historical myth-making that had accompanied the apartheid regime had to be debunked, and the historical record of gross human rights violations set straight. But truth-telling also had to be a medium of demonstrable tolerance: an even-handed preparedness to listen to all sides of the story, and to acknowledge the fault lines between competing perspectives on a much contested past. In so doing, new voice would be given to the victims of gross human rights violations whose stories had previously been excluded from official history-making. The TRC's exercise in negative commemoration had to rehabilitate these voices and legitimize their stories. Truth-telling under the auspices of the TRC was also seen as a strategically and morally preferable option to criminal prosecution of the perpetrators of gross human rights violations, provided they made full disclosures of their wrongdoings to the commission. The TRC, therefore, had to flex its truth-extracting muscle particularly strongly in the case of the perpetrators. Going further still, to produce the desired reconciliation at both the individual and national levels, the commission had to fashion a truth about the past to which all would consent. And it had to be a narrative with a deeply moral message, reaffirming the newfound constitutional commitment to the primacy of human rights.

These multiple aspirations for the power of the TRC's "truth" produced a correspondingly wide-ranging legal mandate to the commission. In some respects, the TRC was asked to undertake a mammoth and complex exercise in historical research. Within a period of two years, it was required to establish as complete a record as possible of gross human rights violations in the country, as well as those inflicted by the apartheid regime beyond South Africa's borders, from 1960 to 1993 (subsequently extended to May 1994), both by examining individual cases and by determining national patterns of violence. The TRC was also mandated to account for these violations by establishing the motives and perspectives of both the victims and the perpetrators. Along with the historical analysis went the requirement of quasi-legal investigation, to assess the veracity and completeness of the disclosures of perpetrators applying for amnesty. In this sense, the TRC proceedings were seen as a substitute/surrogate for a court of law. In addition to the historical research and quasi-legal investigation, the TRC was also expected to function as a public spectacle, by way of victim and perpetrator hearings led by a team of appointed commissioners. These hearings were envisaged as a nation-building confessional, as much as the impartial and authoritative proceedings of a part legal, part scientific committee of experts.

Unlike any prior truth commissions, the TRC was thus set to be both *science* (an accurate and impartial rendition of the country's recent history of gross human rights violations) and *theater* (the public performance of the moral redemption wrought by truth, as a script for the identity of the newly forming, unified South African nation). With the former lay the promise of a robustly objective writing of the past; with the latter came the opportunity to authenticate the stories of hardship, suffering, and marginalization on the part of the victims of apartheid, and to hear the confessions of the perpetrators who wished for forgiveness and reconciliation.

Here, then, was the TRC's dual recipe for negative commemoration. But these different modalities of truth-telling represent distinct discursive domains, norms of evidence, and techniques of validation. The challenge would inevitably lie, therefore, in the extent to which the commission could integrate these into a single, unified, and consistent body of truth, as required by its legal mandate.

THE TRC AS SCIENCE

The greatest proportion of the TRC's time, money, and effort went into its research and investigative tasks. The public face of this fact-finding mission was conducted through the cross-examination of victims and perpetrators during the TRC's public hearings. But the bulk of the work happened behind the scenes, within the ranks of large research bureaucracies created in many different regions of the country.

As suggested earlier, the enabling legislation clearly mandated a serious exercise in rigorous and skilled research and investigation. In line with this intention, considerable powers and resources were placed at the disposal of the commission. Its powers of subpoena, search, and seizure were formidable, far more so than any other truth commission to date. In theory, the commission had unlimited access to state archives that were otherwise closed to researchers. The TRC also had a budget and staff establishment significantly larger than previous state commissions in South Africa, and well in excess of truth commissions elsewhere in the world. This included a sizable research department.

The bulk of the research and investigative work was rooted in the task of taking statements from victims of gross human rights violations. Individual narratives had to be put to the test of independent evidence, often requiring additional research. According to the mandate, the many thousands of individual statements then had to be aggregated into national trends and patterns, along with an effort to provide explanations for these trends, in terms of the motives and causes of people's actions. The promise, however, proved richer than the practice. Members of the TRC research department for the duration of the commission's research work have commented and written about the extent to which the research bureaucracies were poorly coordinated, with little by way of an effectively integrated research strategy to start with.[5] Others point to uneven quality control of the data collected, leading to highly uneven—at times, thoroughly suspect—findings in respect to gross human rights violations.[6] This applied as much to the investigations into the actions of perpetrators (including those applying for amnesty

---

5. See L. Buur, "Monumental Historical Memory: Managing Truth in the Everyday Work of the South African Truth and Reconciliation Commission" and J. Cherry et al., "Researching the 'Truth': A View from the Inside of the Truth and Reconciliation Commission," both in Posel and Simpson (2002).

6. See Piers Pigou, "False Promises and Wasted Opportunities? Inside South Africa's Truth and Reconciliation Commission," in Posel and Simpson (2002).

on the strength of an allegedly full disclosure) as to findings in respect to the fate of victims.

Other limits of the TRC's fact-finding project were epistemologically more fundamental. Indeed, as an exercise in history-writing, the TRC's efforts were seriously flawed in ways that reflected the constraints of the mandate as much as the inefficiencies and ineptitudes of its institutional processes.

The TRC was mandated to produce an historical account using extremely blunt categories of historical analysis. The story of South Africa's recent past was to be written in terms of the gross human rights violations inflicted by perpetrators on victims, in the name of political interests and motives established by the known political organizations of the time. In other words, any facets of the country's history of violence and violation that did not relate directly to the commission of gross human rights violations (as opposed to supposedly lesser violations, such as forced removals from land) and did not fall squarely within the remit of an organization overtly defined as political, fell outside the formal ambit of the commission.

This left the commission ill-equipped to deal with the complexities of the country's history. For example, the apartheid system provoked an uneven, but pernicious, politics of complicity, in which victims of one set of abuses became perpetrators of another, in community struggles that defied the simple moral binary imposed by the commission. This in turn seriously limited the TRC's powers to explain the trajectories of violence within South African communities—a task that "would have required much more finely grained local studies, drawing on larger slices of life history, than the snapshot victim statements that furnished much of the raw material of the report."[7]

---

7. See P. Bonner and N. Nieftagodien, "The Truth and Reconciliation Commission and the Pursuit of 'Social Truth,'" in Posel and Simpson (2002, p. 198).

Another rather extraordinary omission from the TRC's efforts at historical explanation (as required by the mandate) concerns the workings of the apartheid system itself. Although required by the mandate, it was a deep tension within the mandate that lay at the root of the problem. One part of this mandate was to produce a descriptive history of what gross human rights violations had been committed by whom, when, and how. A precise definition of what counted as a gross human rights violation was provided in ways that excluded many of the daily routines of apartheid humiliation and degradation suffered by black South Africans across the board. From this vantage point, therefore, the apartheid system itself was not directly the object of the TRC's inquiry, but merely the background, the political landscape on which the picture of gross human rights violations was to be painted. Yet another facet of the TRC's mandate required that it produce an explanation of *why* gross human rights violations occurred, which required a close investigation of the workings of the apartheid system. The nature of apartheid was simultaneously mere background to the commission's investigations and absolutely central to its findings.

To the credit of the TRC's researchers, many of them urged a stronger engagement with broader structural and institutional features of the apartheid system. A series of so-called institutional hearings were subsequently added to the TRC's agenda of public hearings. Members of the media, business sector, medical profession, legal profession, and faith community were questioned by commissioners, and special hearings on youth, women, and military conscription were also convened.

Unfortunately, notwithstanding the insight and protests of many of the commission's researchers, the TRC's findings shed remarkably little light on apartheid, adding scantily to what was already known. One of the great disappointments of the commission was its failure—for a variety of reasons—to wield the substantial powers of search and seizure conferred on it, to command access to state archives hitherto hidden, in ways that would have unveiled critical facets of the state apparatus and apartheid chains of command.

The TRC's five-volume interim report completed in 1999 (the final report is still awaited) produces something of a narrative on the history of apartheid, but it is fragmented, uneven, and at times inaccurate. Its explanatory powers seriously stunted, this narrative is largely a merely descriptive record of gross human rights violations with very little by way of appropriate contextualization or grasp of the complexities of historical causation.

THE TRC AS THEATER

The most familiar and prominent face of the TRC—nationally and internationally—was its public hearings, a feature unique thus far to this truth commission. These hearings provided a lived enactment of negative commemoration, giving voice to those whose stories hadn't been told, and unrelentingly lifting the veils over the past. Indeed, for most people, the truth uncovered by the TRC is what they saw in the televised versions of these public hearings.

The power of these hearings to proclaim truth lay in the ways in which they staged often grueling and heart-wrenching stories of victimization, along with dramatic confessions and, at times, the spectacle of victim and perpetrator embracing each other in a gesture of mutual redemption and reconciliation. The drama was scripted as an opportunity to construct collective memories of past oppression and struggle, and then to affirm the prospect of reconciliation for the future. Overseen by the charismatic and expressive chair of the TRC, Archbishop Desmond Tutu, many of the public hearings were highly charged emotional sagas, with moments of intense suspense, and lots of tears—often from the chairman himself.

The theater of these public hearings produced—necessitated—very different genres of truth-telling from those of the more scientific efforts at fact-finding. The hearings gave a space for many people to tell their own stories, versions of events that often conflicted with others told in the same forum or which, on closer inspection, were internally inconsistent. Yet none of this seemed to detract from the process of truth-telling. Truth lay in the emotional power of individual stories and the capacity of the hearing to uncover seemingly pristine, uncorrupted narratives of past brutalization and suffering. The spectacle of subjectivity constituted its own evidence; these were stories authenticated by the intensity with which they were told and the immediacy of their telling—as if a public witnessing of the event itself.

This made for excellent television. As one of the leading journalists covering the TRC put it, "The Truth Commission hearings were perfect for television journalism. It was not a story about politicians—it was about the way ordinary men, women, and children felt about the horrors of apartheid. The TV cameras could rake the close-ups of these feelings into every living room in the country, and beyond" (Max du Preez, Executive Producer of the South African Broadcasting Corporation). Indeed, these public hearings were also shown widely on global networks such as CNN and the BBC, bringing the compelling drama of exposé, confession, and at times repentance into the living rooms of people far away, with little if any prior knowledge of South Africa or its past.

The medium, however, powerfully shaped the message, and thereby the kinds of truth that the hearings crafted. If the more scientific fact-finding pursuit commands a careful attention to the details of particular cases, the televised hearings tended to extract more general, universal truths about experience, truths about suffering and victimization, remorse and reconciliation, which undergirded the TRC's moral performance. The televised confessional, which is what the public hearings became, created space for the telling of individual stories, but with an overriding sense of their more global human messages.

This universalizing impulse fundamentally shaped the substance of what was televised, particularly internationally. Globally, the truths constructed about South Africa's recent past were gutted of their complexity and specificity, in efforts to make the suffering of rural South African peasants (for example) comprehensible and persuasive to urban Iranians or New Yorkers. From this perspective, the TRC's exercise in negative commemoration was captured under the familiar rubric of "man's inhumanity to man," a global and timeless story of wrongdoing and the need for moral reparation.

The imperative of nation-building, built into the TRC's mandate, also fashioned the manner of truth depicted in the hearings, in ways that were quite closely aligned with the techniques of truth-telling of the televised confessional. From a nation-building perspective, the factual details of thousands of individual narratives of violation were irrelevant. What mattered was the production of an account of the past sufficient to portray the moral fact of gross human rights violations. For this script, the simple moral binary of victim and perpetrator works perfectly well. There is no need—indeed it would be an unnecessary deviation—to delve into any moral ambiguities and nuances embedded in the politics of complicity or collaboration under apartheid, or to ponder the complexities of social causation.

Good theater, but bad history. Straddling different discursive domains, the TRC's truth-telling practices represented a complex, variegated set of engagements with the past, drawing on multiple sites of confession, narrative accounts, processes of investigation, and sets of data. Contrary to the aspiration contained within the TRC's mandate, these do not cohere as a seamless, unified, and internally consistent body of truth. One of the symptoms of these internal fractures of truth is the way in which the final report is constructed: a disconnected compilation of discrete chunks of information, with little effort at a synthetic unified analysis.[8] What we have by way of a single, unified national history is more of a moral allegory of wrongdoing on both sides, but bereft of a fuller account of how and why this story of violation unfolded as it did.

The final questions, then, are, What does this add up to by way of an exercise in negative commemoration? And does the TRC effectively rebut the paradox of truth in late modernity, in overcoming the widespread philosophical skepticism about the idea of truth that has become so characteristic of our times?

The answers to these questions would differ, depending on the audience to which they are addressed. The chapter concludes by evaluating the truth of the TRC from three different vantage points: the TRC itself (as revealed in its written five-volume report), domestic South African responses, and international perspectives on the TRC.

The TRC's lengthy—albeit historically very truncated—five-volume report contains some extremely revealing reflections on the manner of truth represented by the commission's work. The first is Archbishop Tutu's foreword to the report, in which his rendition of the TRC's accomplishment is markedly more modest and circumspect than the grand, ambitious aspirations of the commission's legal mandate. The report, he claims, offers

> a road map to those who wish to travel into our past. It is not and cannot be the whole story; but it provides *a perspective on the*

---

8. The argument is made more fully in Posel, "The TRC Report: What Kind of Truth? What Kind of History?" in Posel and Simpson (2002).

truth about a past that is more extensive and more complex than any one commission could, in two and a half years, have hoped to capture.[9] [my emphasis]

Tutu's comment reveals a certain hesitancy about the claim to objective truth—but one that is then buried in the rest of the foreword, which retrieves the authority of the commission as an officially trustworthy, suitably impartial, and robust account of the country's recent troubled history. But there are other indications in the text of the report—confirmed by subsequent conversations with some of the commission's senior researchers—that the issue of truth proved to be vexed and conflictual throughout the life of the commission. Indeed, unusually for an official state commission, the TRC report is completely up-front about its overarching epistemological dilemma:

But what about truth—and whose truth? The complexity of this concept . . . emerged in the debates that took place before and during the life of the Commission.[10]

The report also contains an effort to theorize the concept of truth that tries to accommodate some of its complexity. A typology of four different types of truth is proposed, each one proffered to cover a particular facet of the commission's work, and a particular variant of the relationship between objective and subjective renditions of truth-telling. "Factual or forensic truth" was said to refer to the "familiar legal or scientific notion of bringing to light factual, corroborated evidence, of obtaining accurate information through reliable (impartial, objective) procedures."[11] "Personal

---

9. South African TRC Report, vol. 1, ch. 1, para. 5.
10. TRC Report, vol. 1, ch. 5, para. 29.
11. TRC Report, vol. 1, ch. 5, para. 30.

or narrative truth" was seen as "the validation of the individual subjective experiences of people who had previously been silenced or voiceless."[12] Next, "social truth" was "the truth of experience that is established through interaction, discussion and debate."[13] And lastly, the TRC report proffered "healing truth" as truth construed for a particular—healing—purpose, which it considered necessary because "it was not enough simply to determine what happened. Truth as factual, objective information cannot be divorced from the way in which this information is acquired; nor can such information be separated form the purposes it is required to serve."[14]

This conceptual grid was a late addition to the text of the TRC's report, in an effort to put a coherent gloss on the problem that had prompted so much debate, rather than as a framework that had guided the method and substance of the TRC's research and analysis.[15] This is not surprising, since the typology is ultimately unconvincing, even incoherent, and therefore difficult, if not impossible, to apply and use. For example, the differentiation between social and healing truth remains unclear. And the epistemological argument for healing truth—that truth is always contextual and interest-bound—surely undermines the very possibility of factual or forensic truth, as the report defines it. Most significantly, there is no engagement with the relationship between these different types of truth. Is this simply a multiplicity of truths, or do they add up to a coherent, integrated whole? There is no explicit answer. Certainly, there is no formal em-

---

12. TRC Report, vol. 1, ch. 5, para. 36.
13. TRC Report, vol. 1, ch. 5, para. 39–42.
14. TRC Report, vol. 1, ch. 5, para. 43–44.
15. These disclosures were made by scholars who had been researchers in the TRC research department, during the proceedings of a conference on Commissioning the Past: South Africa's Truth and Reconciliation Commission, held at the University of Witwatersrand, June 1999.

brace of a relativistic conclusion, as the TRC's report presents itself with the appropriate authority of an objective, impartial arbiter on the past. Yet the suggested typology of truth remains interesting and significant for what it reveals about how close some members of the commission came to the brink of embracing a multiplicity of truths, and thereby destabilizing the benchmark of objective, integrated truth, which animated the exercise.

Among South African audiences, responses to the TRC's efficacy as the medium of truth and reconciliation have been mixed. Perhaps the greatest success of the TRC—and the site of its biggest impact within the country—has been its role as an historical "lie detector," to use Michael Ignatieff's (1996) phrase. In the aftermath of the TRC, it is no longer possible to dispute the fact that the apartheid regime perpetrated murder, torture, and assault on a large scale, even more in the Southern African region than within the country. Nor is it possible to deny the abuses within the ranks of the liberation movements—even if in each case there is much more to the story than the commission was able to disclose. For Ignatieff, this ought to be enough: "lie detection," he argues, constitutes the essential function of a truth commission. However, the TRC's mandate expected a lot more, in ways that also raised the expectations of its national audiences. The paucity of the commission's rendition of apartheid's "truth"—a source of criticism among academic commentators—has provoked disappointment in many communities with higher expectations of the TRC's propensities to unravel intricate and hitherto opaque local histories of conflict.[16] Some of the victims of gross human rights violations who testified before the commission have expressed their skepticism about the notion of truth-telling as healing,

---

16. See Hugo van der Merwe, "National Versus Local Truths," in Posel and Simpson (2002).

and with that, the promise of reconciliation.[17] And there has been criticism, in legal circles as well as more widely, about the unevenness of the commission's perpetrator findings, particularly in respect to the granting of amnesty. (Other sites of criticism, such as the anger at the state's failure to pay reparations to the victims of apartheid abuses, and the African National Congress' anger at the findings of gross human rights violations within the liberation movement, have less to do with the subject of truth and therefore bear less on the issues at hand than the other responses.)

Significantly, the greatest acclamation and affirmation for the TRC has come from outside the country. Globally, the TRC has been widely hailed as a resounding success, in ways that make it a model for other developing countries to emulate. And it is surely no accident that this verdict on the TRC's "truth" should be passed at the maximum distance from the inner workings of the commission and the complexities of its task. From a global vantage point, the essential truth of the TRC was moral, rather than historical. The TRC—largely through its televised hearings—reaffirmed the tenets of a moral universalism, and its powers to infuse a new democratic dispensation. In the midst of the widespread destabilization and collapse of many developing states, and the continuing eruption of violence, this is a message that the world wants to hear. It vindicates the premises of transitional justice, along with the global impulse to negative commemoration.

It seems, therefore, that positions taken on the extent to which the TRC has rebutted the philosophical skepticism about truth that marked its genealogy would be inversely proportional to their proximity to the inner workings of the commission: the greater the distance from the complexities of the task, the greater the confidence in the rigor and power of the commission's "truth."

---

17. See Pamela Dube, "The Story of Thandi Shezi," and M. Matshoba, "Nothing but the Truth: The Ordeal of Duma Khumalo," in Posel and Simpson (2002).

REFERENCES

Blackburn, S., and Simmons, K., eds. (1999). Truth. Oxford: Oxford University Press.

Fernandez-Armesto, F. (1998). Truth: A History and a Guide for the Perplexed. London: Black Swan.

Hayner, P. (1994). Fifteen truth commissions—1974 to 1994: a comparative study. Human Rights Quarterly 16(4): 597–655.

——— (2001). Unspeakable Truths: Confronting State Terror and Atrocity. New York: Routledge.

Horwich, P. (1990). Truth. Oxford: Blackwell.

Ignatieff, M. (1996). Untitled. Index on Censorship. www.oneworld.org/index-oc/issue596/ignatieff.

Kirkham, R. L. (1992). Theories of Truth: A Critical Introduction. Cambridge, MA: MIT Press.

Posel, D., and Simpson, G., eds. (2002). Commissioning the Past: Understanding South Africa's Truth and Reconciliation Commission. Johannesburg: Wits University Press. (Every chapter in this book deals with the issue of truth, and therefore all bear directly on the questions raised in this essay.)

Rosenau, P. (1992). Postmodernism and the Social Sciences: Insights, Inroads and Intrusions. Princeton, NJ: Princeton University Press.

South African Truth and Reconciliation Commission. (1998). Truth and Reconciliation Commission of South Africa Report, five volumes. Cape Town: Juta & Co.

Steiner, H., ed. (1997). Truth Commissions: A Comparative Assessment. Cambridge, MA: World Peace Foundation.

Taylor, C. (1994). Multiculturalism: Examining the Politics of Recognition. Princeton, NJ: Princeton University Press.

——— (2002). Memory, justice, and inclusion. Paper presented at the Wits Institute for Social and Economic Research (WISER), Johannesburg, June.

United States Institute of Peace Library. Truth Commissions. *www.usip. org/library/truth.html*.

Verwoerd, W. (1996). Continuing the discussion: reflections from within the Truth and Reconciliation Commission. *Current Writing* 8(2).

from *America*

AMERICAN THOUGHT ABOUT TRUTH

———

Douglas Patterson

ARGUABLY THE MOST COMMON use of the words *is true* in ordinary thought and speech in the United States (and, I would think, elsewhere) is their use to concede, contest, or endorse a claim already made. Someone having said, "It was insensitive of Mary not to realize how Elizabeth felt," another might say, "That's not true. How could she have known?" or "That's true, but still, I think she can be forgiven under the circumstances." Saying of something that has been said that it is or is not true allows one to express agreement or disagreement with it without the tedium that would result from repeating the claim in question.

In addition to their service in reducing tedious repetition, the words *is true* greatly enhance the expressive power of one's language, as they allow one to commit oneself to claims that one could not otherwise express. By claiming of things said by others that they're true, I can assert things I could not otherwise assert. On the telephone Kurt says, "*Es schniet im Berlin heute,*" and I say,

"That's true," committing myself to its snowing in Berlin today even if I lack understanding of German. Ellen the classicist says, "'*ebēn*' is an athematic second aorist," and I say, "That's true," committing myself to the claim even if I have no idea what an athematic second aorist is. Deploying the words *is true* thus allows me to commit myself in speech to a great deal to which I could not otherwise commit myself. Likewise the notion of truth is handy when I don't know what someone said but want to endorse it anyway; being very impressed with Ellen's expertise I might well say, "Everything Ellen said in her lecture is true," even if I wasn't there or don't remember what she said, thereby committing myself to various claims about Ancient Greece, making it the case that I spoke in error if in fact Ellen got something wrong.

We can thus say that in the use that has been described here, the inference from a sentence to the claim of it that it is true is always good. If a sentence is something it would be right to say, for example, "Paris is in France," then the claim of it that it is true is also something it would be right to say: since Paris is in France, "Paris is in France" is true. Furthermore, the inference goes just as well in the other direction: if the sentence "John is home" is true, then John is home; it couldn't very well be that the sentence was true when John wasn't home, because the sentence means just that, that John is home.

In characterizing American thought at its most immediate and ordinary, this expressive function of the words *is true* that we have noted is the central phenomenon. However, the use of the words *is true* and the ideas behind it undergo a profound change when Americans are induced to reflect on the meaning of an attribution of truth. The result of this shift is a view of what is said when one says that something is true that is in deep opposition to the unreflective views expressed in practice. This shift takes place most noticeably when ordinary Americans are taken into philosophy classrooms, and so I will discuss the transformation as it takes place there. (Strictly speaking, I make an assumption in what follows: that the students who actually enter the philosophy classrooms I have taught in provide a representative-enough sample that one can draw more general conclusions about everyday American thought about truth from what goes on in American philosophy classrooms. Obviously, American college students are not a representative sample of Americans in many ways, but I believe that in this case the assumption is sound.)

One of the deepest and most characteristic features of the typical American college student's thought about truth is that the inference from a claim to "that's true" and back again, one that comes so naturally in unreflective contexts, is canceled upon reflection. Students, though they might be inclined to assert that wanton cruelty is morally wrong, for instance, will shrink from saying that the claim that it is morally wrong is "true." Once students notice their own hesitancy in this regard, something similar happens when they consider scientific claims, things believed by hearsay, or in extreme cases even claims about the layout of the immediate classroom environment. Many students, once they are asked explicitly to consider whether many of the things they believe are true, become highly averse to claiming that they are. My sense is that the feeling that immediately prompts this hesitancy is that it would be "arrogant" to claim that what one says is true. One can say what one thinks, but it would be overstepping one's bounds to claim, in addition, that what one thinks is true.

This is in direct opposition to the unreflective use of the notion of truth found in ordinary practice, on which a sentence and the claim of it that it is true are quite tightly equivalent; inside the classroom the most common use of the notion of truth is not that one, but rather: "That's true for me, but it might not be true for you." "True for me, but maybe not for you" is intended to mean something more than "I believe that and you might not," but at the same time less than "I am right and you are wrong. What I say is true and what you say is false." Reflective American thought about truth seeks a middle ground between opinion and fact.

This, I contend, is an important key to understanding American political culture. The idea that the crucial axis of evaluation isn't "true or not" but rather "true for me, not for you" encourages by turns the idea that ethical and political debate is irresolvable and that it is morally suspect. In the first instance, since a common standard of evaluation of the truth of claims is denied, there is simply no point in debating anything, and no reason to expect that anything would come of debate. This attitude feeds into the second one, to the effect that to argue with someone about something is somehow to transgress the other's political and moral rights. Many students, in my experience, think that disagreeing with other people, calling what they believe untrue, is positively un-American. The idea seems to be that to say that everyone is entitled to express an opinion is the same as to say that all opinions are equally correct, that nobody can say that anybody else's opinion is wrong—as if the First Amendment to the U.S. Constitution said that there is no objective right and wrong, rather than saying that the government may not hinder people from expressing their views about right and wrong. On this very common American view, disagreement is equated somehow with censorship.

I think, also, that something highly un-American is sensed in saying of what one says that it is true, something related to what American thought finds morally suspect about debate: the un-American sentiment of believing oneself to be better than others. Whatever forms of arrogance and self-promotion Americans are capable of outside the classroom, within it they cling quite strongly to a vision of equality that forbids thinking that one has a less unclouded view of the world than one's neighbor. All of these attitudes are integral parts of the vacuity of American politics, since according to them debate is both pointless and immoral. Think here of the incessant wielding of "partisan" as a term of abuse in the contemporary U.S. Congress. As used there, it means little more than "expresses disagreement about what is best for the country." Presumably the direction of explanation between these attitudes and the institutional arrangements, such as a narrow two-party system, that they support is complicated: the attitudes support the system, although the system, in turn, does not merely by coincidence encourage the attitudes.

Let us call the views about truth and objectivity that emerge in the American classroom "American classroom relativism." Something is seen in the meaning of the words *is true* in American classroom relativism beyond the expressive functions with which I began this essay. If truth were exhausted by this expressive function, it would be no more arrogant to say "That's true" than it is to say "You should varnish from dry to wet" or "Broccoli is delicious"—which is to say it might or might not be arrogant, depending on the circumstances. Where, then, does the feeling of an additional presumption, an arrogance in saying "What I say is true" come from? To answer this, we will do best to ask ourselves what kind of arrogance could be peculiar to speaking. The answer, I believe, is that it is the arrogance of forgetting one's own limitations, of forgetting what one is entitled or qualified to claim. I don't know much, say, about Dutch politics, so I should not presume to speak on the topic.

What presumption could one see in the claim that one's claim is true that one does not see in the claim itself? To say that one's claim is true is, among other things, to say that one is right, that things are as one claims they are. Students who react in the way I am describing see somehow a pretension in saying of what one says that it is true that they do not see in the mere saying of what one says; to say that what one says is true, that one is right in saying it, is to overstep one's bounds. A proper modesty, the student thinks, admits that one is fallible, that one might always be wrong, so one ought not, in addition to saying "Broccoli tastes good" or "It's best to varnish from dry to wet," say that these things one says are true—that would be the arrogance of failing to admit that one can always be wrong.

American classroom relativism recognizes that our view on the world is always partial and prejudicial, and that our views on what is aren't neatly to be hived off from our tastes, our wants, our aversions, yens, and hankerings. It recognizes that because of these things we can easily be wrong in what we believe, that our passions can mislead us and our perspective blind us to some things. Part of our particularity is that we are fallible. However, American classroom relativism draws from this the conclusion that one ought never claim truth for what one says. Does this conclusion follow? As noted, in this moment American classroom relativism breaks the connection, so simple and evident in unreflective contexts, between saying something and saying of what is said that it is true. Roughly, American classroom relativism takes simply saying something to be unproblematically perspectival; one speaks from where one stands. The claim to truth, however, is not a simple repetition of the claim of which truth is predicated; it is taken to be an attempt to occupy the "view from nowhere," to borrow a phrase from Thomas Nagel (1989), a view from beyond particularity and its limitations. To claim that what one says is true is to claim that one has access to how things are that is independent of the foibles of one's own perspective; it is to claim to have transcended the human condition. Since all saying is perspectival, American classroom relativism draws the conclusion that the best one can do is to say of something that it's true from where one stands, true for oneself.

My students are not alone in drawing these conclusions; a good deal of the thought most influential in American humanities departments draws them as well. A good case in point here is Friedrich Nietzsche's (1887) highly influential discussion of truth and objectivity in the third essay of *On the Genealogy of Morals*. Because his influence is so pervasive, a discussion of Nietzsche's views will help us to understand the state of thought about truth in American academia, and to understand the connections of this with American classroom relativism.

Nietzsche argues that scientific ideals of objectivity and the pursuit of truth are expressions of what he takes to be the deep ascetic undercurrent of Judeo-Christian culture, which itself ultimately issues from a turning inward of animal cruelty in the civilizing process:

> Science today has absolutely *no* belief in itself, let alone an ideal above it—and where it still inspires passion, love, ardor, and *suffering* at all, it is not the opposite of the ascetic ideal but rather *the latest and noblest form of it.* [p. 147]

My question is this: What allows Nietzsche to see the pursuit of truth as a form of self-denial or self-abnegation? Whence the reversal of the apparent platitude that one is better off—for example, more likely to succeed in what one does—knowing the truth about how things are?

The source of Nietzsche's views here is an appraisal of the interconnectedness of affect and intellect with which we have seen American classroom relativism about truth agree:

> To see differently . . . to want to see differently, is no small discipline and preparation of the intellect for its future "objectivity"—the latter understood not as "contemplation without interest" (which is a nonsensical absurdity), but as the ability

to control one's Pro and Con and to dispose of them, so that one knows how to employ a *variety* of perspectives and affective interpretations in the service of knowledge.

Henceforth, my dear philosophers, let us be on our guard against the dangerous old conceptual fiction that posited a "pure, will-less, painless, timeless knowing subject"; let us guard against the snares of such contradictory concepts as "pure reason," "absolute spirituality," "knowledge in itself": these always demand that we should think of an eye that is completely unthinkable, an eye turned in no particular direction, in which the active and interpreting forces, through which alone seeing becomes seeing *something*, are supposed to be lacking; these always demand of the eye an absurdity and a nonsense. There is *only* a perspective seeing, *only* a perspective "knowing"; and the *more* affects we allow to speak about one thing, the *more* eyes, different eyes, we can use to observe one thing, the more complete will our "concept" of this thing, our "objectivity," be. [p. 119]

In my experience this is the *only* part of *On the Genealogy of Morals* that my students like, finding as they do Nietzsche's questions about the history of morality unintelligible and his answers to them repugnant. This is not without good reason: what we have in this passage is a registration of the inevitability of intellectual perspective very much of a kind with the ideas that drive American classroom relativism. Nietzsche's criticism of what he takes to be the Western tradition's conception of objectivity is that it requires for its fulfillment a leap outside of one's own skin, and his comments on truth in an essay like "On Truth and Lies in an Extramoral Sense" (1873) make clear that he sees the same connection between this conception of objectivity and deployment of the notion of truth that untutored American thought does:

> The different languages, set side by side, show that what matters with words is never the truth, never an adequate expression; else there would not be so many languages. The "thing in itself" (for that is what pure truth, without consequences, would be) is quite incomprehensible to the creators of language and not at all worth aiming for. One designates only the relations of things to man, and to express them one calls on the boldest metaphors. [pp. 45–46]

> What then is truth? A movable host of metaphors, metonyms, and anthropomorphisms—in short, a sum of human relations, which have been enhanced, transposed, and embellished poetically and rhetorically, and which after long use seem firm, canonical, and obligatory to a people. [pp. 46–47]

I take the first two sentences of the first passage here to be what Nietzsche sees the Western tradition of truth to be, and the rest of the text to be Nietzsche's presentation of what it really is that gets taken for truth. To attain truth traditionally understood would require a leap outside of one's own perspective; what we really have, when we think we have that, are rather various subjectivized aspects of our own experience that we take to be something more. Hence to seek the truth traditionally conceived is to seek to be rid of one's affects and impulses, and because Nietzsche sees these as central to one's identity, the search for truth traditionally conceived is a form of self-denial or self-destruction.

The difference between Nietzsche's thought here and American classroom relativism is that in the *Genealogy* Nietzsche suggests not that we should meekly demur from asserting things, but rather that we should revel in perspective. He seeks to replace what he takes to be an incoherent and self-abnegating conception of objectivity with one that takes the perspectivalist bull by the horns: what we need is not the view from nowhere, but the view from everywhere, or at least from everywhere we can actually get. It is as offered in this spirit that I read the *Genealogy* itself; rather than being the ridiculous exercise in armchair paleoanthropology that to many it appears to be, the work is intended to shake us out of established perspectives on morality by offering some new ones.

However, whether what's said from these perspectives adequately characterizes things as they are, whether it is true, is for Nietzsche not only a matter of indifference, but also something about which no coherent question can really be asked. As with American classroom relativism, the conclusion is that to claim truth is to claim an impossible transcendence of human particularity and perspective. Because these conclusions not only are spontaneously generated by students in American classrooms, but also are very often advocated in the texts that are taught there and by the professors who teach them, I use the term *American classroom relativism* to cover them in both their ordinary and their academic forms.

American classroom relativism is directly at odds with the understanding of truth embodied in the unreflective practice of deploying the words *is true* to concede, contest, or endorse claims already made. According to common and unreflective practice a claim and the claim of it that it is true are always justified or not together; according to American classroom relativism, not only are they not justified together, but the claim of a claim that it is true is never justified. Outside the classroom attributions of truth trip easily off the tongue. Inside the classroom nothing is true because to claim otherwise would be the arrogance of taking oneself to possess the view from nowhere, to be undeceived, impartial, and hence infallible.

How coherent is American classroom relativism? Could we coherently maintain that nothing is strictly speaking true, but that various things are true for various people, that strictly speaking attributions of truth are always relative to a person, a point of view, or something of the sort? There are plenty of places, of course, in which relativism is coherent and indeed appropriate: attributions of simultaneity of physical events are relative to an inertial reference frame, to take one important example, and attributions of time to get to a place are relative to a mode of transit, to take a plainer one.

American classroom relativism about truth would then be the view that *all* claims, not just claims of a particular type, have an important relativization: they're relative to a person, or a point of view. A claim will be true for a person when that person believes that claim. Whether or not this relativization is coherent, it fails to find a middle ground between opinion and fact: so explicated, truth-for is simply defined in terms of belief. Something is true for a person just in case that person believes it. One might as well simply jettison the words *true for me* and *true for you* along with *is true* and simply maintain that one can only talk about what one and others believe, and never about what is true: no question about who is right can arise. Perhaps, then, the real lesson of American classroom relativism is that we simply ought to get rid of the words *is true* entirely.

This might be a view that one can apply to others with impunity; it might be possible to treat another person as the producer of utterances that manifest beliefs while refusing to entertain the question of whether that other is right, whether what he or she says is true. I doubt it, but here I will take what I think is a stronger approach, and ask whether one can coherently adopt this attitude with respect to oneself. I argue that one cannot, as follows. As G. E. Moore (1968) points out, by bringing to our attention what is known as Moore's Paradox, there is a tie between believing something and saying something that appears to be unbreakable. If I say that broccoli tastes good, I can't go on to disavow belief that broccoli tastes good; I cannot say, "Broccoli tastes good, but I don't believe it." This isn't a logical contradiction; after all, since I am Patterson, the claim is equivalent to "Broccoli tastes good, but Patterson doesn't believe it," which is obviously not a contradiction. But if I say, "Broccoli tastes good, but I don't believe it," my hearers will rightly be puzzled or upset. Things go the other way as well: I can't avow the belief that broccoli tastes good and then remain noncommittal when asked whether broccoli tastes good; I may not say, "I believe that broccoli tastes good, but it's an open question whether broccoli tastes good." If I believe it, it isn't an open question for *me*, and I thus may not claim that it is.[1]

So I can't convince myself to believe something without taking what I believe to be the case. If I have determined that I believe that broccoli tastes good, then I have determined (to my own satisfaction) that broccoli tastes good. Believing is thus essentially bound up with taking oneself to be right. In the end this is simply to say that to believe, to take things to be a certain way, is to take them to be that way. This brings us into line with the most common use of the expression *is true*, canvassed at the outset—the use of "true" to express agreement with or endorsement of a claim. If I believe that broccoli tastes good, and must thereby take myself to be right about that, I am committed, given the ordinary function of attributions of truth, to hold of what I believe that it is true, expressing agreement with myself. If I think that broccoli tastes good, then I have to accept that the sentence "Broccoli tastes good" as I understand it is true.

However, this is precisely the point at which American classroom relativism balks, for it sees in the claim that what one has said is true a claim to transcend human particularity and fallibility. I conjecture that this is so because American classroom relativism appreciates the connection between attributing truth

---

1. A good study of this phenomenon is Collins (1987).

to one's beliefs and taking things to be as one takes them to be, and because it believes that taking oneself to be right would be a refusal to recognize human fallibility. Let us clarify this by considering the following three claims:

1. I believe that broccoli tastes good.
2. Broccoli tastes good.
3. "Broccoli tastes good" is true.

Given that he accepts (1), the American classroom relativist doesn't really want to make the step to (2), because he worries that to do so is to take his own belief, expressed in (1), as an infallible guide to how things are. This leaves the connection between (2) and (3) untouched, and since American classroom relativism dictates that one refrain from (2) even when one asserts (1), American classroom relativism likewise dictates that the relativist refrain from (3) as well: one ought not maintain of what one believes that it is true.

The source of American classroom relativism about truth, then, is an attempt to reconcile the attitude of belief with the recognition of fallibility by sundering belief from taking oneself to be right, from expressing conviction that things really are as one takes them to be. This diremption confers upon the notion of truth new content, content it doesn't have in its use merely to endorse claims made, for according to American relativism about truth the claim that one's claim is true is not simply a repetition of that claim, it is the claim that one is right, which American classroom relativism can see only as the claim one's claim is advanced from a standpoint above human limitations.

Thus the reflective beliefs about truth of many Americans are out of accord with their unreflective practice. If American thought about truth is to be reconciled with itself, it must be possible to understand how belief can involve taking oneself to be right, and therefore taking what one believes to be true, without involving taking oneself to be infallible. If this cannot be done, it will not be possible for one to understand how application of the words *is true* can be as it is in ordinary American practice while one simultaneously retains a sane grip on one's own fallibility.

Prima facie there is, in fact, a problem here. Suppose I believe that there are bananas in my kitchen. Doesn't recognizing my fallibility require me to countenance the possibility that there aren't bananas in my kitchen? After all, I have been wrong before. Isn't it possible that I have forgotten that I exhausted my banana supply in a frenzied hunger last night? Perhaps a banana thief is loose in the neighborhood—it just could be so without my knowing. Wouldn't it be, well, arrogance not to recognize these possibilities? And since attributing truth to what I might say is taking myself to be right, wouldn't it be arrogance to say of my utterance "There are bananas in my kitchen" that it is true? What gives me license to think that I'm right in thinking there are bananas in my kitchen?

The problem, however, is that the link between belief and taking oneself to be right, already discussed, won't so easily be broken. Consider the most unreflective sort of belief. At the end of a day or an outing, you return home. In so doing, you act on beliefs about where you live. Do you, in the moment that you board a particular bus, train, or subway, or point your feet, bicycle, automobile, or dirigible toward home, entertain any doubt that you're right in your thinking about where home is? Do you, did you before I mentioned it, entertain any doubt that I am larger than a thimble? (Though you haven't seen me, you did believe me to be larger than a thimble. You surely didn't disbelieve it, and you weren't in a state of uncertainty about it, either. If someone foolishly had offered a wager that I am the size of a thimble, you wouldn't have had to reflect on the case to realize that you were being offered a very good bet.) Such cases can be multiplied indefinitely. We believe, recognizing no possibility that we are wrong, all the time.

Furthermore, when we come to doubt that we are right, we no longer believe. If I really think it's possible that a thief has absconded with my bananas, I no longer believe that there are bananas in my kitchen. I'm relatively sure there are. Being relatively sure isn't believing; it is, at best, believing that it is likely. If I become unsure where I've left my bicycle, I no longer believe that it is near the bookstore; I'm pretty sure it is, I believe that it's likely to be there since that's where I usually put it, but after all I was in a huff this morning. Believing that my bicycle is likely to be near the bookstore isn't believing that it is near the bookstore. Again, such cases can be multiplied indefinitely.

So on the one hand we can very easily be brought to recognize that possibilities of error crowd in upon us from every side, whereas on the other we ignore these possibilities all the time; in fact we ignore them whenever we believe. How do we constantly forget the possibility of error? Is our arrogance (perhaps better: stupidity) this colossal? Following out this line of thought it isn't difficult to see where American classroom relativism about truth comes from—indeed to the vast majority of the students I have worked with, and to many of their professors, it seems inescapable.

American classroom relativism about truth looks inevitable when we think

1. that attributing truth to what one says is saying that things are as one takes them to be,
2. that saying things are as one takes them to be is incompatible with recognizing the possibility of error, and
3. that one is fallible,

for it looks from (1) and (2) as though to claim truth is to claim infallibility, and from (3) that this has to be wrong. The solution hit on by American classroom relativism is to avoid claiming infallibility by refusing to claim truth. Yet this relativism is incompatible with the ordinary use of "is true" to endorse claims made.

The puzzles that drive students to American classroom relativism are not superficial. We would have a way out here if we could see how one could both recognize one's fallibility and claim truth for what one says at the same time. The philosopher David Lewis (1996) runs up against a similar issue in defending his account of knowledge, an account of knowledge that appears to imply that one can know that certain alternatives to what one believes aren't the case simply by assuming that they aren't—that one could know, for instance, that a banana thief hasn't pilfered one's bananas simply by forgetting to wonder whether one has. Clearly, simply allowing this would be unacceptable, would be well past arrogance into stupidity. Here is what Lewis says in his defense:

> Do I claim that you can know P just by presupposing it!? Do I claim you can know that a possibility W does not obtain just by ignoring it? Is that not what my analysis implies, provided that the presupposing and ignoring are proper? Well, yes. And yet I do not claim it. Or rather, I do not claim it for any specified P or W. I have to grant, in general, that knowledge just by presupposing and ignoring is knowledge; but it is an *especially* elusive sort of knowledge, and consequently it is an unclaimable sort of knowledge. You do not even have to practice epistemology to make it vanish. Simply *mentioning* any particular case of this knowledge, aloud or even in silent thought, is a way to attend to the hitherto ignored possibility, and thereby render it no longer ignored, and thereby to create a context in which it is no longer true to ascribe the knowledge in question to yourself or others. So, just as we should think, presuppositions alone are not a basis on which to *claim* knowledge. [pp. 561–562]

The key here is the idea that though one must grant in general that there are possibilities that may be incompatible with some attributed knowledge, one cannot claim this of any *particular* possibility, for to claim it of a particular possibility is to cease to ignore that possibility. Hence one can never claim to know something that one merely assumes.

When we turn to belief and focus on the most basic, unreflective cases, we find that we recognize no possibility of error, though when we reflect upon ourselves, obviously there are many possibilities of error—many "counterpossibilities"—we find that we were unreflectively ignoring. Are we, in our unreflective moments, taking ourselves to be infallible? Following Lewis, we may deny this, for to recognize one's fallibility one need only recognize that there may be counterpossibilities to what one believes, that some of one's beliefs may be false. One needn't grant, of any particular possibility, that it is a counterpossibility to a particular belief; that is, one needn't grant of any particular belief that it may be false for some particular reason. For to do this would be to take it that there are live possibilities that what one believes is false, and to do this, in turn, by the above considerations, is to cease to believe: if there really are counterpossibilities that I recognize to what I once believed, I have come merely to believe it to be likely, probable, possible, or something of the sort, that what I believed was true.

Thus, to take myself to be fallible I need only believe that I may have beliefs that are mistaken. I do not need to believe that there are counterpossibilities to my belief that there are bananas in my kitchen. To recognize one's fallibility is to endorse the claim "Possibly, I have a belief that is not true." This should not be confused with the claim "I have a belief that is possibly not true." One's reasons for believing the first needn't be reasons for doubting any of one's present beliefs; they need only be reasons of the sort under discussion here for recognizing the limitations of one's ways of forming beliefs and the perspectives to which these limitations give rise. One's reasons for believing the second, by contrast, will only be reasons for thinking some particular belief possibly false, and to recognize such reasons is to lose the belief.[2]

The difference between "Possibly, I have a belief that is not true" and "I have a belief that is possibly not true," though in fact profound, is superficially subtle, since ordinary thought lacks the habit of paying close attention to differences such as that between "Possibly, there is something such that . . ." and "There is something such that possibly . . ." There are many other examples of such inarticulateness when it comes to the order of important expressions. I used to ride the train from Pittsburgh to New York with some regularity, and during this ride I was informed over the loudspeaker that in Harrisburg "All doors will not open." Taking the claim literally, one wonders why the train stopped at all. Of course, the intended claim was that not all doors would open in Harrisburg, and everyone on the train took it that way. No harm came in this instance. The shift that gives rise to American classroom relativism is similar, though its consequences are more profound. It is as if in the classroom the conclusion were drawn that it is impossible to get off the train in Harrisburg. If we recognize the difference between "Possibly, I have a belief that is false" and "I have a belief that is possibly false," we can reconcile our unreflective deployment of the words *is true* with our reflective grasp on our own fallibility; if we don't recognize the difference, American classroom relativism is the result. In the charged

---

2. This simplifies a bit. I ignore the possibility that one might be informed, as if by an oracle, that one has a false belief without being given any information about which belief it is. In the ordinary run of cases the only reason for believing that one has a false belief is a reason for believing that some particular belief is false. Nothing material in the text is affected by this simplification in formulation.

environment of the classroom, the difference is simply ignored under the pressure to recognize human fallibility and avoid arrogance, and classroom thought simply grants that in order to recognize "Possibly, I have a belief that is not true," one must commit oneself to the consequences of "This belief of mine is possibly not true" where "this belief" is whatever belief is salient in the discussion that raises the issue of fallibility and hence the confusion of "Possibly, I have a belief that is not true" and "I have a belief that is possibly not true."

This, then, is the way out. To recognize one's fallibility one need not grant the possible falsehood of specific beliefs—which is good, since one cannot do that. When we arrive at this conception of what it is to take oneself to be fallible we see that taking oneself to be fallible is entirely compatible with recognizing no possibilities that any particular one of one's beliefs is false. It is thus compatible with the deep link between believing and taking oneself to be right, and of this with taking one's beliefs to be true, that we have examined above.

American classroom relativism about truth is thus unnecessary for an appropriate modesty; it takes it that the only way to recognize fallibility is to refuse to take oneself to be right, to refuse to insist that there are no counterpossibilities to what one believes—and to do this, we have argued, is to cease to believe. The source of the opposition to itself that untutored American thought falls into in reflection about truth is thus a misunderstanding of what it is to recognize one's own fallibility. One can recognize one's own fallibility while taking oneself actually to be right, and thereby taking what one believes and says to be true.

I maintain the same for the academic branch of American classroom relativism. To believe is to take a stand on how things are. I cannot see Nietzschean perspectivalism as something that leaves each perspective something I can recognize as genuinely a stand, or if it is genuinely a stand, genuinely my own. In the end I think this speaks to what it is to have a mind, or to be a person; it speaks to integrity. I can't believe, or sincerely say, incompatible things, because I have only one perspective, one location in intellectual space just as I have only one location in physical space. Being "of two minds" on something is a state in which I sometimes languish, but this is the destruction of perspective, not its multiplication; when I am of two minds about something, it can't be said that I have a perspective at all. If I don't have one at all, I don't have more than one.

As I have already made clear, I believe that classroom relativism among students is a real and honest response to genuine difficulties. It thus seems likely that there is more than mere logical inarticulateness behind American classroom relativism. What makes it so easy for individuals to fall into the understanding of fallibility that gives rise to American classroom relativism when those same people won't draw the conclusion, from the verbal conflation of "all will not" and "not all will," that one can't exit the train in Harrisburg? Is there anything particularly American behind it?

To answer these questions requires a kind of interpretation of American thought that must remain highly speculative. Here is one hypothesis. The American aversion to opinion and debate greatly diminishes the American student's sense that to believe is to take a stand on something, since taking a stand, claiming that what one says is right, that it is true, is precisely the object of American aversion, seeming as it does to many Americans to be both un-American and immoral, a failure to live and let live. Hence, when American thought about truth and belief encounters the prima facie incompatibility of the recognition of one's own fallibility and taking what one believes to be true, American thought is happiest to release the tension by denying the link between believing and taking one's beliefs to be accurate, the link, from one's own perspective, between (1) and (2) in the list on p. 43.

We can perhaps trace these difficulties in understanding perspective and fallibility back to the ultimately political and practical problems of understanding what tolerance and pluralism, the keystones of America's vision of itself, amount to. (Note that I do not say that they are keystones of America's actuality, though of course America's vision of itself is part of its actuality.) The creation of a tolerant, pluralistic society requires that the energies of dogmatism and various totalizing understandings of the human condition be corralled and tamed. Yet if one really takes oneself to be right about how people ought to live, why ought one accept the limitations on one's capacity to implement this vision in one's world imposed by the demands of tolerance for other visions of the good life? What motive could one have to be tolerant of what one takes to be error, indeed, moral error? An easy way out of the problem is to replace intolerance in one's political vision with relativism in one's moral vision. The belief that values are not absolute, that one's conception of the good life is "true for oneself" but maybe not "true for others" is the easiest and most readily available solution to the practical political problems of toleration and pluralism; if people can be persuaded to abandon the belief that their vision of the good life is normative for others, the difficulty of reconciling competing conceptions of the good life with a pluralistic political order is set aside.[3] The cultivation of relativism about truth, then, is a practicable response to the demands of pluralism, and it is the one that has come to work in America. As I have noted, it doesn't cohere well with ordinary practice with the words *is true*, but in the reflective contexts where people consider whether their own

---

3. Many of the formulations here deliberately invoke the thought of American political philosopher John Rawls (1972, 1993).

visions of how to live are valid for others, it provides an easy argument for tolerance.

This mismatch between theory and practice parallels and is part of the mismatch between theory and practice many find in the failure of American policy to live up to the ideals of pluralism and tolerance on the international stage, and that many see in the distance between American ideals and the persistence of racism, sexism, and homophobia in America. Just as relativism about truth tends to stay behind in the classroom, so, too, do the ideals of pluralism and tolerance, liberty and justice for all to which it lends some facile support. These failures in America should not be exaggerated—the history of tolerant political orders is the history of a tradition needing to be reminded again and again of its failures to live up to its conception of itself— but they are quite real, and they are accurately reflected in the charges of American "hypocrisy" heard in many quarters of the world.

A pluralistic political order founded on relativism about truth might well be stable over the long haul. Such an order is threatened not by a factionalization that might tear it apart, but by a kind of political stagnation in which private individuals withdraw to an ever greater degree into gated communities and office parks and leave management of the political realm ever more fully in the hands of a supposedly neutral bureaucratic technocracy. If the point of the government is to get out of the "values" business, then one can keep one's values at home and let the government pursue its supposedly neutral ends. I won't shock many when I assert that this is rather clearly the fate that America currently faces, with its nearly identical political parties, empty electoral contests, and epidemic nonvoting. At a deep level, this will not change without a weakening of the grip on the American mind of the relativistic idea that political and ethical debate are pointless and immoral. I wouldn't say that America's political problems could be straightened out merely with a little more clear thinking about the philosophical interpretation of truth and fallibility, but I will say a change in views on these topics will be a part of any renaissance in the American political sphere.

This, at any rate, is one interpretation of the sources and sustenance of American classroom relativism that strikes me as having some plausibility, and that sees something particularly American behind the prevalence of relativism about truth in America: the need to live up to American ideals of toleration. Perhaps the other essays in this volume will help us to understand whether there really is anything peculiarly American here.

REFERENCES

Collins, A. (1987). *The Nature of Mental Things*. Notre Dame, IN: University of Notre Dame Press.

Lewis, D. (1996). Elusive knowledge. *Australasian Journal of Philosophy* 74.

Moore, G. E. (1968). A reply to my critics. In *The Philosophy of G. E. Moore*, ed. P. A. Schlipp. Open Court Publishing.

Nagel, T. (1989). *The View from Nowhere*. New York: Oxford University Press.

Nietzsche, F. (1873). On truth and lies in an extra-moral sense. In *The Portable Nietzsche*. New York: Viking, 1954.

——— (1887). *On the Genealogy of Morals and Ecce Homo*, trans. W. Kaufmann. New York: Vintage, 1967.

Rawls, J. (1972). *A Theory of Justice*. Cambridge, MA: Harvard University Press.

——— (1993). *Political Liberalism*. New York: Columbia University Press.

from the Arab World

**ASSENT AND TRUTH IN THE MEDIEVAL ARABIC
PHILOSOPHICAL TRADITION**

———

Ali Benmakhalouf

Translated by Robert Bononno

TRUTH AND HARMONY

DURING THE MIDDLE AGES, Arab-language philosophy underwent a period of unprecedented development. Scholars like Jean Jolivet have claimed that philosophy was "born twice in Islam" at this time: "first, as an original theology, *kalâm* [literally, "speech"], then as a philosophical movement that was largely based on Greek sources."[1] This phenomenon is all the more remarkable when we consider that philosophy, drawn from Greek sources, did not seek the protection of theology, which could be said to be its initial form. It explicitly constituted itself as a philosophy based on the Greek pagan tradition, but it sought its justification in law. It was used to interpret revealed texts that had a juridical content and drew its legitimacy from them, as Averroës

---

1. Jolivet (1995, p. 407).

indicated at the beginning of his *Decisive Treatise*. Access to the truth implied the use of the Aristotelian syllogism: "Since it is well established that divine law requires that we apply rational speculation to considerations of the universe, since reflection consists only in determining the unknown from the known, to draw it out, which is the syllogism, or is accomplished by means of the syllogism, we are obligated in our speculations about the universe to use the rational syllogism."[2] Leo Strauss has drawn attention to this. There is, in fact, something unique to Arab and Jewish philosophy in that they always situate truth in reference to the court of law: "For the Jew and the Muslim, religion is primarily not, as it is for the Christian, a faith formulated in dogmas, but a law, a code of divine origin. Accordingly, the religious science, the *sacra doctrina*, is not dogmatic theology, *theologia revelata*, but the science of the law, *halaka*, or *fiqh*."[3]

There was a twofold effort at reconciliation: the reconciliation of the sacred text with the pagan philosophies of Plato and Aristotle, and the reconciliation of those pagan philosophies with one another. The truth could not be multiple, but the access to truth could. To legitimate the study of pagan texts, it was necessary to harmonize them to overcome the objection that these philosophies contradicted and thereby negated one another. The challenge of harmonizing these truths is what animated medieval Arab philosophers.

Averroës believed that alone one could not have access to the whole truth. Only the succession of generations and the acknowledged continuity among different cultures could provide an image of it: "It is our duty, should we find, among our predecessors of an earlier time, a considered theory of the universe, consistent with the conditions that demonstration requires, to

---

2. Averroës (2001).
3. Strauss (1989, p. 221).

examine what they have claimed in their books."[4] Since no truth contradicts another, the attempt to harmonize different philosophies with one another and philosophy with the sacred text was undertaken. Al-Farabi wrote a *Philosophy of Plato and Aristotle*,[5] a text in which he reconciles the Platonic dialogues and Aristotle. For this, it is necessary only that "philosophy revolve around the question 'as' and 'in a certain relation to.'"[6] It is therefore possible to read Aristotle's *Organon* as the realization of Plato's program expressed in the myth of the cave: "And the example Plato gives in his book *The Republic* when discussing the cave—how man leaves the cave and then returns to it—is adapted from the order Aristotle gave to the parts of logic."[7] The *Categories* is considered a treatise on the first elements of thought and the *Analytics* as the most perfect work. It was only gradually, following Plato, that the science of demonstration found in the *Analytics* was acquired. Plato had spoken of the internal dialogue of the soul with itself; Arab philosophers, following Aristotle, placed reasoning—the demonstration of proofs—within this logos. For al-Farabi there could be no conflict between Platonic truth understood as the goal to which the effort of remembrance strives and Aristotelian science, which assumes that all teaching, given or received, results in "an understanding that exists already."[8] The lack of harmony arises only from an imperfect understanding of the doctrines of the two thinkers.

Similarly, the debate on the universality or particularity of Aristotelian categories has led to a number of misunderstandings. Grammarians like Sirafi opposed the idea that Aristotle's categories were universal. They were unrelated to our universal ways of

---

4. Averroës (2001).
5. Al-Farabi (2001a).
6. Al-Farabi, op. cit.
7. Al-Farabi, (1971, p. 213).
8. Al-Farabi, op. cit.

thinking, regardless of our linguistic schema; they were merely a codification of the Greek language. The school of al-Farabi, which included scholars like Abu Bishr Matta (932), defended the universality of these categories by showing that they were universal intelligibles. The issues were significant, for what was at stake was the question of whether we have access to a single truth through concepts shared by all or if concepts vary depending on the people and, consequently, whether whatever is said about those concepts and, therefore, the truth vary as well. If Matta's thesis is valid, it is not only possible but desirable to teach Aristotle, since he was able to categorize intelligibles shared by all humanity. If Sirafi's thesis is valid, then Aristotle's categories are not universal and it is possible to dispense with their teaching and concentrate on the codification of the Arab language while looking for a specific mode of thought that characterizes it. The dialogue between the grammarian and the logician was related by Abu Hayyan al Tawhîdî (985) in his book *Plaisir et Convivialité* (the eighth night).

The demonstrative paradigm has captured the attention of all the Arab philosophers who have commented on Aristotle's *Organon*. In al-Farabi, just as with Avicenna and Averroës, the science of the Aristotelian syllogism has served as a model of understanding. It is a unifying principle even in fields such as poetry and rhetoric.

FROM THE SYLLOGISTIC TO THE POETIC: MULTIPLE PATHWAYS TO TRUTH

The demonstrative paradigm has been contextualized in a theory of knowledge that accounts for different degrees of consent. In this way these philosophies have developed an organon throughout their commentaries, that is, an organon that integrates rhetoric and poetics. The work of Deborah Black has shown the influence of this expanded logic on all language acts. The syllogism has been recognized as a general method comprising the demonstrative syllogism as well as the rhetorical enthymeme or poetic metaphor. The enthymeme is a syllogism in which we elide a premise, and the metaphor can be understood as a syllogism that supplies only its conclusion and leaves it up to the listener or reader to reconstruct the two premises and participate in the creation of the metaphor, since this figure is complete only when the addressee participates in its construction in one way or another. The integration of rhetoric and logic is generally based on two arguments: (1) recognition of the rudimentary rationality present in the multitude, which, not having access to the truth through demonstration, has access only to what resembles truth, an object of rhetoric; however, what resembles truth "among the people assumes the place of truth[9]"; (2) although the multitude does not have access to the truth, it is disposed to understand it: "People are well disposed by their nature to understand the truth itself and, in most cases, intuit the truth and act accordingly."[10] Although the multitude is satisfied with what resembles the truth, it is not however condemned at this step; it is the responsibility of the science of logic, the science of truth, to account for what is similar to the truth, for the substitution that occurs between them, and which can only take place according to the norms of the true.

Ibn Ridwân (died 1061 or 1068) summarizes this five-part differentiation of truth according to the nature of the syllogism. There is a

> demonstrative discourse by which we attempt to obtain one of two things, perfect representation or certainty; a dialectic discourse through which we also try to obtain that which gets

---

9. Averroës (1986).
10. Averroës, op. cit.

the upper hand in opinions of representation and belief; a sophistical discourse that assimilates the false to the true as we assimilate the false dinar and adulterated dirham to the good dinar and true dirham; a persuasive discourse on which the soul rests and to whose content it is subject; a poetic discourse that engenders in the soul the understanding of the thing based on what is similar to it and what imitates it.[11]

This concern for rhetoric and poetics presents not only an intellectual challenge but a religious one as well. It not only indicates multiple paths to the truth but also provides Arab philosophers with the ability to read the sacred text in a way that harmonizes it with the methods of philosophy. When Averroës comments on Aristotle's poetics, he doesn't hesitate to use examples that are consistent with both Aristotelian ideas and Arabic-Muslim culture. So, when Aristotle evokes Oedipus's killing his father and marrying his mother as an example of tragedy, Averroës makes a religious transposition and indicates that this case is formally identical to the case of Abraham sacrificing his son, or of Joseph tormented by his brothers. In all these cases (Oedipus, Abraham, Joseph), an unwarranted misfortune befalls someone who is noble or has carried out some noble action.

Averroës went on to construct a theory of the receptivity of the Koranic text in which Aristotelian distinctions and Koranic distinctions are reconciled. There are three forms of assent taken from Aristotle: rhetorical, dialectical, and demonstrative. The poetics discussed above does not appear among these three forms, for it does not imply assent; metaphors as well as images exhort the public to pursue something or to avoid it. These three forms are presented as methods engendered by the sacred text itself. Averroës quotes the verse in which he claims to find these three forms: "Call

---

11. Ridwân (1977, p. 202).

them to the path of your Lord with wisdom and words of good advice; and reason with them in the best way possible" (Sura 16:125). Wisdom is compared to philosophy, exhortation to rhetoric, and reasoning to dialectic. Wisdom is manifest in the power the elite possesses to demonstrate the verities; rhetoric concerns the crowd and not the elite; it is used to persuade the crowd about those things it needs to be convinced of. It is consistent with the interests of the polity for it is entirely suitable to the consent required by power to obtain social cohesion. Rhetorical consent is characterized by the immediate inclination to something without giving credence to views that contradict this consent, even with respect to possibility. In other words, it does not, like dialectic, present us with arguments to weigh, a method of evaluation pro and con. Dialectic allows this. But its polemic function has been misused by theologians, for rather than concentrating on the manner of acquiring principles and ensuring conviction, they convert dialectics into sophistry. Dialectics then destroys cohesion, becomes something essentially negative. It entails the practice of defending propositions by destroying contrary propositions, in conformity with "that logic whereby the adversary is chased into a network of questions with only two responses, whereby the ways of escape are continuously narrowed."[12]

Additionally, dialectic was shifted toward rhetoric, that is, something that can convince without further examination and is claimed to involve the highest form of understanding. Al-Farabi writes: "As for the intellect that theologians are always talking about, claiming 'this is what the intellect shows,' or 'this is what the intellect denies,' or 'the intellect admits this,' or 'the intellect does not admit this,' they mean by that only what is acceptable for everyone upon first impressions."[13]

---

12. Monnot (1983, p. 9, quoted by Jolivet, 1995, p. 410).
13. Al-Farabi (2001, p. 66).

In the best of cases the dialectic of the theologians provides only an opinion that approximates certainty but is not certainty (*Résumé des Topiques*, p.151). Dialectical discourse consists of widely known premises, and such premises give rise to belief based on the testimony of everyone or the greatest number, but it is not based on the nature of the thing itself, contrary to what occurs in the case of demonstration. Dialectical consent is based only on the fact that others share the same opinion but not on the fact that opinion is knowledge of something. It follows that dialectical premises can be false. It also follows that they have no specific subject but, like rhetoric, form a predicate and a subject not by being modeled on their composition outside the soul—that is, not according to what things are in themselves—but only on what is commonly acknowledged about those things.

Averroës introduces a well-argued critique of induction to rebut the arguments of the theologians. This involves demonstrating that in the case of induction our certainty is not as great as with the syllogism: all bodies are created since most of those we know have been created. This gives rise to the conclusion that the world was created because it is a body. With induction we move from the particular to the universal; with the syllogism, one of the premises is necessarily universal. With induction the power of reasoning is that of the syllogism of the first figure, but without the universal premise: "Air, fire, earth, and water are bodies; these bodies are created; therefore all bodies are created" (the example is used to rebut the creationism of Asch'arite theologians). Moreover, assuming that the induction is complete, it does not tell us if the predicate is related to the subject by necessity; it's possible that their relation is accidental. In our example creation might be an accidental characteristic of the body. That is why induction can only claim belief in what is held in common. Induction used for demonstration can only serve to point us in the direction of certainty without producing it.

There is a significant difference then between what is used to guide us in demonstration and what is used for its own sake.

In the middle commentary to the *Peri Hermeneias*, the distinction between the dialectic and the scientific approach is clearly brought out; the first allows for homonymy in questions, the second does not (Aristotle). The dialectician does not ask *what it is*, he does not look for the essence, does not, therefore, have to avoid homonymy; his only goal is to obtain from his interlocutor, with whom he shares the same knowledge, one of two contradictory statements in order to drive him toward contradiction. For example, is all pleasure a good or not? We have two members of a contradiction: pleasure is a good, pleasure is not a good. The respondent need only supply one of the two answers for the questioner to push him toward contradicting himself. For one of the two, the game consists in getting the other to acknowledge either of the two premises, for the other in not doing so. The question is not about the nature of pleasure. The goal is refutation, even though the one who is made to contradict himself can always say he does not understand pleasure in that way and refuse to be driven toward the absurd position intended by the questioner. As a result there is a polemic charge associated with dialectic. It can give rise either to greater homonymy of meaning or to a common search for univocity of meaning, and therefore to a reduction of homonymy. Dialectics can in the best of cases serve as a preparation for science in the sense that it enables us to turn a topos into a premise likely to appear in a syllogism, but most of the time collapses into argument and yields only preferences rather than understanding.

The various ways of showing belief serve to justify the existence of the manifest and the hidden in the sacred text. Therefore, nothing is intrinsically manifest or hidden, for meanings are uniquely dependent on the receptivity of the text: "It is for this reason that the meaning of the revealed text is doubled as an obvious meaning and a hidden meaning. The obvious comprises the symbols employed for such concepts and the hidden comprises those concepts that are discovered only by those who know demonstration."[14] So to address a question through demonstration to someone who cannot understand it results in infidelity[15]; we manage only to raise doubts and weaken faith, without providing the means for argument. In short, we engage in bad dialectics and pseudo-demonstration. It is in this field that theologians excel. Infidelity is the result of a mismatch between the method exposed and the public to whom it is addressed.

PRACTICAL TRUTH

Those Arab philosophers involved in practical philosophy did not have access to Aristotle's *Politics*. They wrote commentaries to Plato's *Republic* based on original readings of the text. For al-Farabi[16] reconciliation of Socrates and Thrasymachus was necessary: one possessed the science of virtue and the other was able to address the young to educate them. According to al-Farabi, Plato had shown that

> Thrasymachus was better qualified than Socrates to form the character of the young and instruct the greatest number; Socrates had only the capacity to conduct a scientific investigation of justice and virtue, and the power of love, but he did not have the ability to shape the character of the young or the greatest number; and the philosopher, the prince, and the legislator must be able

---

14. Averroës (2001).
15. Averroës, op. cit.
16. Al-Farabi (2000).

to use both methods: the Socratic method with the elite and the Thrasymachic method with the young or the greatest number.[17]

The advantage of al-Farabi's analysis is that it acknowledges that the man of knowledge, the philosopher, is in danger in a corrupt city and that there is great urgency that the political education of the greatest number be carried out to safeguard truth. He therefore assigns to Plato the reform of ways of life so that truth can manifest itself. Speaking of Plato, he adds the following comment: "He again evokes the greatest number of citizens of the cities and nations of his time. He affirms that the perfect man, the man who searches, and the virtuous man, are in grave danger. We must find a means for the greatest number to change their way of life and their opinions and embrace truth and the virtuous way of life, or move in that direction."[18] This revisionist reading of Plato shows al-Farabi's concern in not limiting philosophy to the city state. The philosopher is not an ascetic who has withdrawn to the mountains of thought. Just as he must work to transform his internal discourse of demonstration into an external discourse accessible to others, he must also participate in the gradual transformation of opinions of his city so that the truth can find a favorable context for manifesting itself.

Averroës, in his *Middle Commentary on Plato's Republic*, also reconciles the positions of the philosopher and the imam. The imam in Arabic is the one who serves as a guide. But Plato taught that only the philosopher can serve as a guide. The idea of a legislator-philosopher, therefore, is given credibility as someone who possesses the virtues described by Plato and those the Muslim community is prepared to recognize in the person who is able to serve as the voice of the sacred text. Philosophy is the royal

---

17. Al-Farabi (2000).
18. Al-Farabi, op. cit.

art that creates happiness for philosophers and laymen guided by philosophers. As soon as the philosopher lives in a political society, he is unable to escape the situation created by the naturally difficult relations between the philosopher and the layman. The sociopolitical context is unfavorable to philosophers when the adepts of religion adopt the images present in the sacred text without seeing them as signs of the speculative ideas discussed by philosophy. If a nation adopts a religion, al-Farabi says, without seeing that that religion depends on a philosophy, if it therefore adopts religious content without connecting it to "speculative things that are justified in philosophy by means of reliable demonstration,"[19] then it may arise that "the adepts of philosophy are forced, for their own safety, to oppose the adepts of religion."[20] It is important to note that the opposition in question is merely a form of polemic that does not have the virtue of dialectics, which can be used to grasp shared principles. It is not an opposition to religion but to the belief "professed by its adepts, for whom religion is contrary to philosophy."[21]

This integration of Greek philosophy in the Muslim context was not always accepted. There were two notable opponents to this undertaking, the philosophers al-Ghazali (d. 1111) and Ibn Taymiyya. Al-Ghazali deplored the fact that the young had substituted Greek philosophy for the study of the Koran and the tradition of the prophet. It was not that they were opposed to learning this philosophy, but they felt it was necessary to choose between logic, a good tool capable of being reused, and metaphysics, which was a deviation from knowledge. He rejected the introduction of necessity within natural phenomena and the four Aristotelian causes. Blending a form of empiricism with the reestablishment

---

19. Al-Farabi (1970, p. 149).
20. op. cit.
21. op. cit.

of theological teaching, his criticism of Avicenna is primarily a critique of creation as emanation. For al-Ghazali the emanation of the world as an uninterrupted flux threatens divine transcendence: God must be thought of as separate from his creation in conformity with the teachings of the sacred text. Al-Ghazali, in his "Inconsistency of the Philosophers," refutes the argument about the eternity of the world, an argument that philosophers like al-Farabi and Avicenna had drawn from Aristotle and had strengthened by insisting on divine immutability. God's will cannot change from moment to moment; therefore, there cannot be a moment when God decides to create the world, and thus the world is ancient, persistent, and composed of eternal matter. Al-Ghazali rejected this type of argument, which seemed to him an extreme rationalization of divine will, which is in reality unfathomable. His criticism is based on empiricist assumptions: there cannot be any necessity in things; even time is only a way for us to represent succession. The argument that claims we cannot acknowledge the creation of the world since we would have to acknowledge a time before time, a time before the simultaneous creation of time and the world, presumes time as a metaphysical reality, whereas it is only a mode of human representation. Al-Ghazali's empiricism is evident even when he accounts for realities that are not accessible to the intellect. For him there is another domain, where mankind can turn a visionary gaze to realities his intellect is unable to grasp, but this domain is best understood by analogy with empirical experiences such as sleep. For mankind sleep is the experience of a vision that is not dependent on the data of sensation. "God has given his creatures in the experience of sleep an example of prophecy. A sleeper may have dreams of what will happen, sometimes clear in meaning, sometimes symbolic, which can be explained by interpretation."[22]

---

22. Al-Ghazali (2001, p. 98).

In this way al-Ghazali can account for the reality of prophecy by the method of analogy, which deduces the reality of a suprasensible domain from a sensible domain. Using both syllogism and analogy, al-Ghazali borrowed what he claims to be a neutral tool from Greek philosophers, deductive reasoning, and at the same time made use of analogy to insist on the reality of a domain that escaped demonstrative understanding.

More critical of Greek philosophical ideas was Ibn Taymiyya (b. 1263), who even rejected the syllogism. Since the start of the tenth century, the syllogism had been the only way of achieving proven and necessary understanding. Ibn Taymiyya[23] hoped to relativize this paradigm of understanding.

REVEALED TRUTH AND PHILOSOPHICAL TRUTH: THE IMPOSSIBLE DUALITY

Ibn Taymiyya also refused to accept that there should be no more than two premises. The number of premises should vary depending on the needs of the person. To limit the number of premises to two, therefore, is arbitrary. Support for this is based on the existence of the enthymeme, which elides a premise because it is obvious. The discussion finds a practical outlet in the relation of the syllogism to the universal propositions of sacred texts. The fact that alcoholic beverages are prohibited is something Muslims know; they don't have to arrive at this conclusion by means of a syllogism. Some may doubt the status of intoxicating beverages, such as those made from a base of honey, dates, and so on. But these need only refer to the words of the prophet: "Everything that is intoxicating is

---

23. Hallaq (1993).

prohibited." Thus the prophet has answered Muslims by means of a universal proposition without having to resort to a syllogism:

>   Everything that is intoxicating is an alcoholic beverage.
>   All alcoholic beverages are prohibited.
>   Everything that is intoxicating is prohibited.

This reasoning must be adapted to the person being convinced. Depending on his state of knowledge, we may have need of one of the two or even more than two premises. If someone does not know that alcohol made from dates is an intoxicating beverage and, therefore, is prohibited, then he will need only two premises. However, the situation may arise where someone knows that a particular beverage is intoxicating and that everything that is intoxicating is alcoholic, but may not know that the prophet forbids alcoholic beverages, because such a person may have been raised among heretics or have recently converted. That person may know that the prophet has said, "Everything that is intoxicating is forbidden," and that this particular beverage is alcoholic, and that the prophet has forbidden alcoholic beverages, but may not know that the prophet is the messenger of God and that the messenger has forbidden all Muslims to drink such substances. The person may think that the prophet permits the consumption to some Muslims, of whom he is one, or that the prophet permits their consumption for medical reasons. It is not sufficient for such a person to know that wine, for example, is categorically forbidden. He needs to know that it is intoxicating, that it is alcoholic, that the prophet forbids what is intoxicating, that Mohammed is the messenger of God, and that, therefore, he forbids what God forbids.

Also claiming a form of radical empiricism, Ibn Taymiyya considered the distinctions between the essential and the accidental to be arbitrary and the requirement of a universal premise in a syllogism to be factitious. These distinctions between essence and accident are not conventions for Ibn Taymiyya; they express a choice that holds one thing for essential and another for accidental. Ultimately, and consistent with the empirical method already made use of by al-Ghazali, human knowledge is related to the intentions of the speakers and the language they use to classify the things they claim to know. The challenge is to reestablish the epistemic legitimacy of something belonging to the prophetic tradition, a transmission that cannot be reduced to the form of a syllogism. The analogical process is preferred to the syllogism for it is based on the use of particular cases that are within the scope of our understanding, for man is a creature who cannot claim to share with God the pleasure of active thought. Averroës had, following Aristotle, recognized the possibility for man's intellect to coincide at rare moments with divine thought. Ibn Taymiyya and al-Ghazali are skeptics, who believe that man cannot attain the truth using rational tools. Only revelation, transmitted by prophetic tradition, provides an uncontested source of truth. The truth, ultimately, is a function of its source rather than its validity or justification. It is caught up in the web of authority of prophetic tradition and escapes those who attempt to circumscribe it through demonstration.

The problem raised by al-Ghazali and Ibn Taymiyya's questioning of philosophy can be formulated as follows: If the *Corpus aristotelicum* is to be taught as the true method, revealed law is relegated to the status of an allegory of absolute truth. This goes beyond the model of reconciliation between Aristotle's philosophy and Koranic wisdom seen above. In this case Aristotle's philosophy would not simply be an allegory of revealed truth but just the opposite; Aristotelian methodology itself would be used to determine what is worth or not worth questioning. Al-Ghazali and Ibn Taymiyya understood, and rejected, the challenge of a pagan philosophy that presented itself as a paradigm of knowledge. It is up to us to ask how the philosophers who fought for the paradigm in its demonstrative form, that is, the philosophers who made syllogism the exclusive tool of knowledge, were able to account for revealed truth and prophetic transmission.

Aristotle, in the *Topics*, cautions us not to try to demonstrate the truth of things that are far removed from us like the existence of miracles. Averroës respects the injunction to avoid constructing fictional accounts about origins that some may accept at face value: "The ancient philosophers don't talk about miracles because, according to them, miracles are among those things that must not be examined or questioned. These are principles of law and whoever examines them or doubts them must, according to them, be punished, such as, for example, someone who examines all the principles of legislation."[24] In this way Averroës strongly criticizes the Avicennan attempt to try to account for prophetic imagination. The transfer of this question from the theoretical to the practical shows that for Averroës the prophet is above all a legislator rather than a scholar. His imagination is speculative like the intellect. It is analogous to the true dream. But there is nothing more to say about it.

The imagination, on the other hand, which is tied to knowledge, is the same imagination as Aristotle describes in book III of "On the Soul." This imagination is dependent on sensation and provides the intellect with imaginative forms that are the origins of our concepts of things. But how can we legitimate an imagination whose content resides outside the senses? Rather than provide a status to an imagination illuminated by the divine without the help of the senses, an imagination that would thereby explain the advent of miracles, Averroës turns to the forms of intelligibility accessible to mankind. The Koran is a text

---

24. Averroës (1987, p. 515).

written in a language capable of being deciphered by everyone. We must therefore concentrate on the sense inherent in the sacred text and not speculate about its material constitution as a text or the prophetic substrate this text assumes. "Concerning that which [al-Ghazali] says of the vision of the prophets, among the ancients I know only Ibn Sinna (Avicenna) to have spoken of it. What the ancients say about revelation and visions is related to God through the mediation of a spiritual, not a corporeal, being, the donor, according to them, of human intellect; which is what our contemporaries call the agent intellect and what the scriptural text calls an angel."[25] In emphasizing the receptivity of the Koran, Averroës makes use of Mu'tazilite arguments. The Mu'tazilites were known as being rationalist theologians who defended the claim that God can speak only in a human language understood by those who listen to him. And by translating the agent intellect, the active intellect that in Aristotle actualizes intelligibles, into religious terms (angel), Averroës erects gateways between the philosophical reading and the religious reading, while sidestepping the problem of dramatizing the very controversial question, in its theoretical formulation, of the prophetic imagination.

Avoiding a philosophy of religion while providing both philosophy and religion with a status is the challenge presented by rationalists like al-Farabi and Averroës. Whereas Averroës, as we have seen, reverses what others have theorized, al-Farabi uses the hypothetical-deductive method to put the relation between religion and philosophy into perspective, which does not result in a philosophy of religion. He examines the fictional case of a people who received religion without realizing that

---

25. Averroës (1987, p. 515).

their religion "followed a perfect philosophy," and uses religious "illustrations" to demonstrate the truth of things: "Whenever religion follows a perfect philosophy, when the theoretical realities that are found in it are not instituted in the same way they are in that philosophy, using words that serve to express them and which are only expressed by their illustrations . . . we cannot be certain that this religion will not contradict philosophy, that its followers will not challenge the latter and dismiss it."[26]

To better understand the relation between the truths inferred from philosophy and those given by religion, we need only consider geographic movement to obtain an idea of the universality of conceptual schemas. Not only would it be contradictory to believe that there is a religion's truth and a philosophical truth, but also dividing a truth will certainly lead to its destruction. Truth is unified but its expressions are varied. We can have access to the truths of nature without having been raised in a religion. This is represented by the fiction, presented by Ibn Tufayl, following Avicenna, of a man living alone on an island, who is raised by a gazelle. The confrontation of his natural understanding acquired through adaptation to his environment and observation with knowledge transmitted to him by Asal, the man raised in religion, who lands on the island, illustrates the seamless compatibility between what religion transmits and what the universe teaches. But conflicts arise when we try to transmit the truths of nature to the greatest number. Hayy, having returned to Asal's civilized world, must confront the lack of harmony between the status of truth and the grip of prejudice: "Hayy ben Yaqzân thus undertook to instruct them and reveal to them the

---

26. Al-Farabi, (1970, p. 155).

secrets of wisdom. But he had barely risen somewhat above the exoteric meaning to address certain truths contrary to their prejudices, when they began to drift away from him. Their souls rejected the doctrines he presented and, while putting on a good face out of courtesy for a stranger and out of consideration for their friend Asal, they grew annoyed with him in their hearts."[27]

THE TRUTH ACCORDING TO MUSLIM LAW

Everywhere in the Koran there is found a vocabulary of proof (the *bayinât*) and a lexicon of affirmation (*shahada*). There are different degrees of acceptance or admissibility of testimony: "Just as the testimony of he who is not upright is not admissible, corrupt information is not accepted. It remains without value. For although the words *information* and *testimony* are different, they are semantically associated in the majority of cases. This is why information from someone who is without morality is inadmissible for men of science, as is his testimony."[28]

Muslim jurisprudence is distinct with respect to the privilege accorded its texts. The judge, in Muslim procedure, must refer to the Koran, to the sayings of the prophet, and to the consensus of the community in order to judge the facts. Of course he also takes into consideration the testimony of witnesses, sworn oaths, the refusal to swear an oath, and avowals, but he is not subject to the facts alone. It is not the facts that pressure the judge to speak the truth but the interpretation of the texts:

> Unlike the canon law judge or the judge of common law, the qâdi does not have to discover the truth in the facts. He finds it

---

27. Tufay (1999, p. 135).
28. Johansen (2000, p. 47).

in the texts. He has the duty to "judge on the basis of truth and law" (al-qada' bil'haqq) but the truth is represented in the forms of an uncontestable knowledge (ilm yaqîn), which has three sources: 1) the revealed word of God, the Koran; 2) the interpretation of that word by the normative practice of the prophet (sunna), which proceeds from the historicization of the Koran and has been inspired by God, and 3) the consensus of religious scholars.[29]

From an epistemic point of view, how can we understand this preference for the text over the fact? We can begin with the distinction between *de re* and *de dicto* beliefs. *De re* beliefs refer to real things as they occur. If I believe that someone has committed a crime, my *de re* belief signifies that I am capable of indicating the culprit or making a complaint to the police. *De dicto* belief is a referred belief, obtained within the framework of the dictum. It is an element of language and, as a result, is unbound from the actual circumstances of speech, which is not the case with *de re* beliefs. Also, it is more easily attached to procedural knowledge than *de re* belief, which assumes reference to a speaker. So if truth is to be discovered in texts and not in facts, based on the quotation given above, it is important to realize that the truth of a text is easier to inscribe in procedural knowledge than the truth of facts, which assumes, through testimony, knowledge of the facts themselves, even though our knowledge is based on testimony and not on facts.

Legal texts are well known to religious scholars. The judge can consult a scholar, the mufti, a man who is a specialist in law and whose opinion, therefore, is authoritative. He has an exhaustive knowledge of Muslim law that is not found in the ordinary citizen, but his advice is not subject to any real sanctions. Muftis

---

29. Johansen (1996, p. 148).

are often appointed by government administrators to assist the judges, who are the only ones qualified to interpret the law.

Additionally, no decision by a judge results in jurisprudence on its own; it is always possible to judge differently. This gives rise to the notion that divergence among legal doctrines has been considered positive and even encouraged by the words attributed to the prophet: "The difference among the doctrines in my community is the sign of God's grace."[30] Doctrines are controversial, as well as certain sources of law, such as legal reasoning by analogy (*qiyas*), the personal effort of interpreting the law (*ijtihâd*), or in some cases consensus (*al-ijma'*), namely the synchronic aspect of the living tradition that characterizes each generation, and finally the preponderance given to one text over another (*al-tarjih*). Only the Koran and the sayings of the prophet (*sunna*) are not subject to such qualifications. However, even here controversy can arise over the precedence of one over the other. Although the two texts are complementary, for the great majority of religious scholars, Koranic law cannot be understood without considering the practice of the prophet. The forms of access to juridical truth through a reading of these texts can be broken down as follows: (1) The sayings of the prophet can emphasize a Koranic injunction like that against bearing false witness. (2) They can specify the general propositions of the Koran as statements about charity, pilgrimage, and so on. (3) They can complement the Koran in certain respects, as for example the forbidden forms of marriage.

According to Averroës, the subdivision of the sources of juridical norms in the Koran, the prophetic sayings, consensus, and analogical reasoning, has a nested structure in which each part is justified by that which comes before it, the Koran remain-

---

30. Johansen (1996, p. 149).

ing the fundamental text that limits the infinite regression. Thus, the sayings of the prophet are considered a source of law, for the sacred text says to follow the prophets; consensus is elevated to the rank of a source since the prophet has legitimated it through his sayings; and syllogistic derivation and analogical reasoning are as well because, depending on these three sources, they are among the sources of the law.

How did Averroës inscribe an appreciation of the last source of law, namely syllogistic activity, within this order of priorities? He had to show that it was through this activity that the objectives of the other principles of law were clarified. The parentage between the paradigm of knowledge, which is the demonstrative syllogism, and the legal paradigm that is constituted by analogical reasoning, is illuminating. It indicates a rational prejudice in all human activity, theoretical or practical, whether it concerns metaphysics or law. The Koran and the sayings of the prophet are not monolithic blocks that can simply be repeated to achieve understanding; they themselves respond to rational criteria. If syllogistic derivation relies on these three other sources of law, it is because they lend themselves to it; in other words, they lend themselves to a derivation of meaning that may only involve a word, which is to say, a metaphor, or an entire proposition, which is to say, a syllogism. It remains to be seen how these multiple derivations are carried out.

In the Koran there are redundant and implicit expressions, metaphors such as "the faith requires," "prayer prevents evil," "the wings of vice," and so on. It is false to claim that, to the extent the Koran is a true statement, it could not contain metaphor, since metaphor can be more appropriate than the literal expression, not because it introduces a new meaning but because it makes new use of an old meaning. Moreover, the frequent use of a term such as *metaphor* is no longer metaphoric; it is the sought-for intention from the point of view of communication (*al takhâttub*) that is relevant. This is the case with metaphoric expressions such as "Dead [things] are forbidden to you," "Your mothers are forbidden to you," "Your daughters are forbidden to you." These three statements blend the implicit and the metaphorical, and refer respectively to the injunction against eating meat that has not been sacrificed according to ritual, and the injunction against incest with one's mother or daughter. The intention is carried by the intended action: eating in one case, sexual congress in the other.

The derivation of meaning is also related to a complete statement. The use of the enthymeme, the rhetorical syllogism lacking a premise, comes into play here as well. In the verse "Those who are ill or traveling, as many days," which has the form of an enthymeme, a premise is missing. Rewriting it, we get: Those who are ill do not fast some days during Ramadan, but must fast throughout the entire month of Ramadan; thus they will have to fast later for as many days as they did not fast during the month of Ramadan. Without the rewording, which functions tacitly in the listener, the norm is incomprehensible.

The legal syllogism, therefore, is essential to legal practice. "It is one of the fundamental elements of jurisprudence"[31] as the three other sources attest.

In the sayings of the prophet, the *sunna*, there is also a justification of syllogistic derivation. The prophet determined usage from the point of view (*ra'yy*) of the *ijtihâd*, the effort of interpreting the sacred text. The argument is as follows: How can something that was sanctioned by law during the time of the prophet and of revelation fail to retain that status once the period of revelation is over?[32] One of the sayings of the prophet reads: "I judge you according to the point of view [found] in material where there is no revelation." And the Koran corroborates the use of judgment

---

31. MM, p. 19.
32. Ibid.

and with it the search for reasons that can ground a syllogistic derivation. One of the verses that supports this point of view reads: "The book has been brought down to you in truth so you might judge among the people according to what God makes you see."

The third source of law is consensus. This is divided into two components: those things about which scholars and the common people agree, as is the case with ablution, prayer, fasting, and charity, and those that are the result of consensus among scholars without the support of the masses, as with theoretical questions. Ordinarily, in the Muslim tradition, consensus is a form of community agreement regarding the meaning of religious texts. Averroës indicates that there can only be consensus about practical questions, not about theoretical matters.[33] Transposed from the legal to the theological framework, consensus loses all signifying scope; the practice of theologians, based on interpretations that claim to be consensual and that do not allow room for the growth of sectarianism, is badly shaken. The philosophical culture in which Averroës worked pushed him to foreground proof, not consensus, and to abandon this concept for the dialectic of the theologians. The task was made even easier by the fact that we coexist with the source of law in a human field that is neither divine (the Koran) nor prophetic (the sayings of the prophet).

Averroës devoted an entire work to *al-khilâf*, or legal controversy. This type of problematic privileges the use of the syllogism in a form that is both generic and specific: generic like the derivation of meaning or a proposition, specific in the canonical form of the Aristotelian syllogism. Averroës's contribution[34] to

---

33. Averroës, French translation, p. 125.
34. "His intended and avowed goal is to try to find a valid and likely explanation for this Khilâf [controversy] by studying the methods for deducing these solutions from classical sources of law. Contrary to his predecessors in this undertaking . . . although Malikite and from a family of important Malikites, his ambition was never to introduce a sense of polemic to this literature; he

jurisprudential analysis is the fusion of the tradition of the *fiqh* (the foundations of Muslim law) and the Aristotelian tradition.

It should be noted that the concept of legal controversy is considered by Averroës as a positive element that enables us to perfect the critical use of reason. Legal controversy is contrasted, point by point, with theological dissension. Far from trying to produce a new dogma, legal controversy indicates the scope and limits of each legal solution and appeals to the informed judgment of the reader, who through his efforts (*al-ijtihâd*) is able to form his own opinion. Obviously, it is not a question of encouraging people to disobey the law under cover of expressing their opinion. But it is important to have a means for comparing several juridical models, associated with various schools of law, while remaining aware that the boundary between the believer committed to his faith and the citizen obedient to the law is not clear in a religion of law like Islam. The use of the legal syllogism is justified in Averroës by the following argument: the situations that occur being indefinite and sources, such as the Koran, and the sayings of the prophet, being limited, new cases should be derived from a consideration of those that are known. Legal reasoning (*qiyas char'i*) is based on an analogy with four components: (1) the base case, (2) the related derived case, (3) the cause or resemblance according to which the legal qualification is made, and (4) the judgment (*hukm*) or legal qualification. Starting from the original case provided by the texts (Koran, prophetic sayings), a transference to the related case is made (new situation for

---

was engaged in the defense of his school. He honestly and objectively reproduced every valid point of view on any important question, accompanied by his own arguments, or rather those that seemed most pertinent." See *La place d'Averroës Juriste Dans l'Histoire du Malikisme et de l'Espagne Musulmane*, in A. Turki, p. 286.

which there is no established jurisprudence) when they share the same cause, both cases being considered as likely to be proportionate, even equivalent.

Legal reasoning, as probable as it is, can present important challenges. For example, extending the scope of a term beyond its explicit reference in the Koran. This is the case when only the man is mentioned and the judge decides to consider that the woman also benefits from the same rights.

It is therefore reasonable to consider the technical or logical lacunae in Muslim law. They are technical when it is only a question of extending, generalizing, or interpreting the law. They are logical when an effort of juridical creation is required. In all cases confidence in human rationality, no matter how rudimentary, is a criterion for retaining law's conciliatory role in society.

REFERENCES

Alami, A. (2001). *L'ontologie Modale, Étude de la Théorie des Modes d'Abû Hashim al-Gubba'i*. Vrin.

Al-Farabi. (1970). *L'épître des particules*, ed. M. Mahdi. Beirut.

——— (1971). *Didascalia in Rhetoricam Aristotelis*. Beirut.

——— (1999). *L'Harmonie Entre les Opinions de Platon et d'Aristote*, French trans. Institut Français de Damas.

——— (2000). La philosophie de Platon, son ordre, ses parties. *Revue Philosophie* 36.

——— (2001a). *Alfarabi: Philosophy of Plato and Aristotle*, trans., with an introduction by M. Mahdi, with a foreword by C. E. Butterworth and T. L. Pangle, rev. ed., selections, in English. Ithaca, NY: Cornell University Press.

——— (2001b). *L'épître sur l'intellect*, French trans. by D. Hamzah. L'Harmattan.

Al-Ghazali. (2001). *Deliverance from Error and Mystical Union with the Almighty, al-Munqidh min al-dalal*; English trans. with introduction by M. Abulaylah; introduction and notes by G. F. McLean. Washington, DC: Council for Research in Values and Philosophy.

Averroës. (1986). *Middle Commentary on Aristotle's Poetics*, trans., with introduction and notes, by C. E. Butterworth (Talkh¯is kit¯ab al-shi'r). Princeton, NJ: Princeton University Press.

——— (1987). *Tâhâfut al tâhâfut*, 2nd ed. Beirut: Bouygues.

——— (1998). *Middle Commentaries on Aristotle's Categories and De Interpretatione*, trans., with notes and introduction by C. E. Butterworth, (Talkh¯is kit¯ab al-maq¯ul¯at), in English. South Bend, IN: St. Augustine's Press.

——— (2000). *L'islam et la Raison*. GF.

——— (2001). *The Book of the Decisive Treatise Determining the Connection Between the Law and Wisdom; and, The Epistle Dedicatory*, trans., with introduction and notes, by C. E. Butterworth, (Fasl al-maq¯al f¯im¯a bayna al-shar¯i'ah wa-al-hikmah min al-ittis¯al) in English and Arabic. Provo, UT: Brigham Young University Press.

——— (2002a). *La Béatitude de l'Âme*, French trans., Vrin.

——— (2002b). *Middle Commentary on Aristotle's De Anima*, a critical edition of the Arabic text, with English trans., notes, and introduction by A. L. Ivry, 1st ed. (Talkh¯is kit¯ab al-nafs), in English. Provo, UT: Brigham Young University Press.

——— (2003). *Commentaire Moyen sur la Rhétorique d'Aristotle*, French trans., Vrin.

Benmakhalouf, A. (2000). *Averroès, Figures du Savoir*. Belles Lettres.

Black, D. L. (1990). *Logic and Aristotle's Rhetoric and Poetics in Medieval Arabic Philosophy*. E. J. Brill.

Hallaq, W. B. (1993). *Ibn Taymiyya Against the Greek Logicians*. Clarendon Press.

Johansen, B. (1996). Vérité et torture: ius commune et droit musulman entre le Xe et le XIIIe siècle. In *De la violence*, ed. F. Héritier, p. 148. Odile Jacob.

——— (2000). Muslim, *Sahih*. I, 7, quoted by H. Touati, *Islam et Voyage au Moyen Âge*, p. 47.

Jolivet, J. (1995). *Philosophie médiévale arabe et latine*. Vrin.

Leaman, O. (1985, 2002). *An Introduction to Classical Islamic Philosophy*. Cambridge: Cambridge University Press.

de Libera, A. (1999). *L'Art des Généralités*. Ch. IV Avicenne. Aubier.

Mahdi, M. (2000). *La Cité Vertueuse d'Al-Farabi*. Albin Michel.

Monnot, G. (1983). *Les Doctrines des Chrétiens dans le "Moghni" d'Abd al-Jabbar*, Mélanges de l'Institut Dominicain d'Études Orientales, vol. 16.

Munk, S. (1988). *Mélanges de Philosophie Juive et Arabe*. Vrin.

Ridwân, I. (1977). *Livre sur ce qui est utilisé de la logique dans les sciences et les arts*, manuscript established by Maroun Aouad, "La doctrine rhétorique d'ibn Ridwan et la didascalia in Rhetoricam Aristotelis ex Glosa Al Farabii." In *Arabic Sciences and Philosophy*, vol. 7.

Sebti, M. (2000). *Avicenne, l'Âme Humaine*. Philosophies, no. 129. PUF.

——— (200x). *Philosophies Arabe*. Philosophies, no. 77. PUF.

Strauss, L. (1989). *The Rebirth of Classical Political Rationalism: An Introduction to the Thought of Leo Strauss: Essays and Lectures*, selected and introduced by T. L. Pangle. Chicago: University of Chicago Press.

Tufay, I. (1999). *Le Philosophe Autodidacte*, French trans. L. Gauthier. Mille et une Nuits.

From China

ON ZHEN

———

Yang Guo-rong

Translated by Wang Bin

THE IDEOGRAPH-WORD 真, pronounced as Zhen, is designated by translators and sinologists alike as the Chinese counterpart of the English words *true* and *truth*. This semantic correspondence is problematic and sometimes misleading, though the stress on some overlaps do facilitate the project of communication across linguistic boundaries. Take, for example, two English expressions: "a true story" and "real life." Here the two adjectives are not interchangeable, whereas their Chinese versions are identical: 真实 Zhenshi, a compound word meaning Zhen. In other words, Zhen incorporates two ideas that have to be separated in English by "true" and "real." Why is it that a story cannot be "real"? This is not an easy question even to many advanced learners of the English language in China. The difference between "true" and "real" or, if we could paraphrase their respective meanings, between "what is represented" and "what actually exists" involves a big story about cultural difference. In the final analysis, Zhen could not find its equivalent in English any more than "true" or "truth" could locate its own in Chinese. Nevertheless, this is too true to be a good argument. This essay takes the conventional correspondence between "Zhen" and "true" as a point of departure as well as a converging topic for further exploration. Another thing we should point out in advance is that Zhen can be a noun and an adjective without any morphological differentiation. This distinctive feature at the lexical level is characteristic of all Chinese ideograph-words, naturally and necessarily affecting the use of Chinese words, including Zhen, at the syntactic level. Though structural arrangement and meaning creation are interrelated, we will not discuss morphological problems. The focus here is on the semantic aspects of Zhen working within the context of Chinese culture.

First, Zhen often points to what can be taken as empirical fact, as opposed to what is false. It is in this sense that Zhen corresponds to the word *true*. But, the cognitive tradition in China tends to add something more to what is propositionally true: an axiological power thought of as intrinsic to the propositions concerned. We shall deal with this problem later. Second, Zhen in everyday conversation is often used to describe a moral behavior or personality, similar to the English expression "sincere" and standing in contrast to "hypocritical." When attention moves to metaphysical concerns, Zhen refers to what is real or reality, as in the sense of philosophical ontology. Closely linked to the third sense of Zhen is its interest in the ultimate Being. Finally, Zhen also signifies the "authentic nature" in the sense of aesthetics, contrary to what is artificial. All these semantic aspects often work together, and it is difficult to isolate one from the others without some miscomprehension of the use of the word. An analytical investigation of Zhen, however, has to distinguish senses, situations, and concerns so as to show more specifically how the word is used to structure and restructure Chinese cultural life.

ZHEN: FACTS AND AUTHORITY

In the perspective of Anglo-Saxon analytical philosophy, Zhen, meaning "true," presupposes the relation of what is uttered to what the utterance refers to. It is a matter of relationship between words and things or language and reality. In the Chinese intellectual framework, the problem arising from Zhen, meaning "true," is more "epistemological" than glossocentric. It emphasizes the possible correspondence between facts and ideas about those facts rather than the word–thing relationship. It leads, through metaphysical speculation, to the unity of reality and mind, which is traditionally described as "the combination of Heaven and man." I put "epistemological" in quotation marks because, in pursuit of facts, what is further stressed is not the operation of the cognitive faculty as the necessary and logically a priori condition in the Kantian sense, but a general attitude of mind toward what one wishes to know. Such a desirable attitude is summed up in Confucius's work and accepted by the Chinese: "Shall I teach you [the way to acquire] knowledge? To say that you know when you do know and say that you do not know when you do not know—that is [the way to acquire] knowledge" (*The Analects*, 2:17). It is further specified in the process of knowing: "Confucius was completely free from four things: he had no arbitrariness of opinion, no dogmatism, no obstinacy, and no egotism" (*The Analects*, 9:4). Apparently, the principle set by Confucius does not tell us how to acquire knowledge in the sense of modern scientific methodology. It only teaches us that if we wish to know the true or the fact, we should preclude subjective preoccupations and respect the object of knowing. It is a down-to-earth spirit popularly called "seeking truth from the facts." It well matches local pragmatism, calls attention to practical things, and encourages a desire for quick success. In passing it explains in part why the Chinese success in dealing with the physical world in the past two thousand years is more technological than scientific.

"Seeking truth from the facts" also finds expression in the exegeses of ancient classics. Hermeneutics as a discipline in China started and flourished as early as the Han Dynasty (206 B.C. to 200 A.D.), and reached its academic summit in the Qing Dynasty (1644–1912). It constitutes the main body of traditional scholarship in the domain of the humanities. "Facts" here refer to the authenticity of the philological details—orthographic, semantic, or phonetic—contained in the documents to be interpreted. From the very beginning, the project of interpretation was motivated by contemporary politics with a view to promoting or undermining the predominant ideology. Some scholars might highlight facts, whereas others would play up truths drawn from facts, but all were agreed that the classics themselves must presuppose a system of truth manifest in their arguments. In other words, those principles advocated by the five Confucian classics, namely *Book of Odes*, *Book of History*, *Book of Rites*, *Book of Changes*, and *Spring and Autumn Annals*, were regarded as universally true and therefore immune to any doubt or criticism. The study of the classics only means explanation of the universal truth contained in them. "To study the classics necessarily excludes any refutation of the classics," as a scholar from the Qing Dynasty put it. Since the classics obtained the authority of telling true from false, people would appeal to them when they disagreed in terms of juridical controversy or academic contention. Even trivial disagreements in everyday life might depend on those classics for solutions. Then, the truth proved to be a fixed dogma, whereas facts were relegated to what the canonized writings told us.

The study of the classics with respect to "seeking truth from the facts" has cultivated not only an academic convention but a way of thinking in that respect. Since then, confrontation between two sides in China, reformists versus conservatists, or revolutionaries versus reactionaries, or Marxists versus anti-Marxists, has always displayed an identical pattern: each side has its own classics as the source of truth upon which one can rely so as to dismiss the other as false or wrong.

ZHEN: IDEAL AND PRACTICE

To a large extent social ideals in the Chinese context relate to past experience rather than just future possibilities. More often than not, a particular ideal could work on people because it was accepted as something historically true. Otherwise put, historical memories sublimate into a strong belief which, in turn, stimulates activities for the realization of that past dream in contemporary life. In this respect, classical Confucianism played an important role, providing an illustration par excellence.

Confucius once made a thorough investigation of the social/political institutions adopted respectively by the three dynasties chronologically before him: Xia, Shang, and Zhou. He hesitated to assess Xia's and Shang's political systems in default of cogent documentary evidence but was convinced that Zhou's system of rites as a way of government was perfect: both historically true and contemporarily pertinent. When confronted with the morally chaotic status quo, his lifelong ambition was a self-conscious commission: an attempt to restore Zhou's system of rites. "How complete and elegant are its regulations! I follow Chou." With this declaration he went from one state to another, taking pains, though in vain, to persuade political leaders to follow his social ideal and conform to what was supposed to be universally true. The response to his sincerity was contempt, indifference, humiliation, and vilification. His belief in Zhen never wavered; he turned frustration into a positive force that pushed his political career forward. He never won a single politician to his view, but his influence in terms of the formation of social ideals has proved powerful and persistent in the history of Chinese sociopolitical life.

Mencius took over Confucius's noble project and continued his predecessor's search for Zhen. He did not go back directly to Chou's system of rites for inspiration and schemata. Rather he managed to highlight the notion of Ren (仁) as his social ideal. Ren has been variously translated as benevolence, love, human-heartedness, and altruism. One may well render it as humanity or the basis of all goodness. Mencius advocated "government by Ren"—humane government. But when he delineated the content of "government by Ren," Mencius resorted to the agricultural institutions of the Zhou Dynasty, thus adding a dimension of historical reality to Ren as a social ideal. Mencius was also famous for his argument that history proceeded in a cycle, with a period of order and a period of chaos succeeding each other and that every five hundred years a sage-king would arise to put the world in order. In his mind, the recurrence of humane government by such a sage-king had been true before and would become true again in the future. Obviously, it was through a forged identity between social ideals and historical facts that belief in Zhen (truth) could lead to such a political persuasion. This is very much characteristic of Chinese political culture in general.

In parallel with what is supposed to be factually true in history, Zhen also works as a moral principle by which to regulate practice in real life with a view to maintaining humane government. Two conceptions are primordial in understanding and implementing that principle: an "enlightened king" (明君) and "clean officials" (清官). The first represents a sage-king who must be open-minded about disagreements, respect facts even though they might jeopardize his own interest, and let promotion strictly be based on merit and abilities. The second conception demands, on the part of the king's subjects, honesty, decency, and insusceptibility to corruption. Even now people still turn to this moral principle for a criterion by which political leaders and public servants are to be assessed. On top of that, a real gentleman in society is a person, most probably an intellectual, who dares to speak up for the sake of Zhen in that sense, even at the cost of his life.

ZHEN AS SINCERITY

What constitutes one's "real self"? How can one attain an ideal personality? How does that self or personality work and manifest itself in all kinds of intersubjective events? These questions lead us to another dimension of Zhen: sincerity in cultivating human goodness.

There are two diametrically opposed motivations, according to Confucius, for the establishment of the ideal personality. The first subjects one to external judgment, whereas the other only follows the dictates of one's own conscience. Heteronomy gives rise to hypocrisy, whereas belief in the real self alone leads to sincerity. Both *The Great Learning* and *The Doctrine of the Mean*, the well-known Confucian canons, stress the importance of sincerity in one's self-fulfillment. Those arguments that relate sincerity to self or personality reflect the attempt to internalize ethic norms and, at the same time, naturalize the product of that internalization, ideal personality or the real self, as Zhen. It is said that the local literati used to compare the spontaneous fondness of beautiful colors to one's pursuit of genuine goodness, hoping to locate an intrinsic source for the sincerity of moral acts. In short, good behavior, according to Confucianism, comes from inner virtue whose Zhen (genuine sincerity), in turn, guarantees its goodness. This is not merely basic to Confucianism proper; it prevails over the whole Chinese moral tradition.

Complementary to Zhen as sincerity is the Taoist understanding of Zhen as "nature." The ideal personality is described as "Zhen person" (真人), pointing to a human existence in accordance with Nature, and Lao Zi, the father of Taoism, is regarded as a "Zhen person" par excellence. As the famous Taoist maxim puts it, "Follow Heaven and appreciate Zhen." Here "Heaven" stands for the natural course and "Zhen" implies an ideal life for human beings. In this Taoist context, therefore, pursuit of Zhen means return to Nature, the original state of affairs uncontaminated by man-made civilization. "Artificial" rather than "hypocrisy" is the opposite of Zhen. Then, Taoist Zhen, at least in theory, amounts to a rejection of Confucian Zhen, since they have different understandings of what is real, genuine, or true: nature for Taoism and culture for Confucianism. In intellectual life, however, they are highly complementary, providing a strategy of legitimizing a dual personality cultivated exactly within that Confucian-Taoist antithesis. It is common knowledge in China that the Chinese intelligentsia, in history and at present, often advocate Confucian-styled sincerity when politically successful but return to Taoist Zhen for spiritual shelter or self-identity if frustration seems overwhelming. A double strategy is always at hand: active participation and retirement from the world. There is no lack of a well-prepared discourse for its legitimacy. Going both ways, one believes that he is always right in terms of Zhen.

Though different in attitude toward the nature/culture problem, both Confucianism and Taoism emphasize spontaneity in terms of the manifestation of Zhen. According to Confucianism, good behavior is an effortless, off-hand expression of one's conscience without any intention of gaining favorable appraisal or pleasing social conventions. It is the moment when the mind is free of external restrictions but never transgresses the internalized moral law. To put it in another way, when the superego (morality) becomes part of the unconscious, its control comes naturally from the mind itself. This is the sublime of Zhen as sincerity. Spontaneity in the Taoist perspective presents quite another picture. It excludes any attempt at the internalization of moral law and disregards regulations set by social conventions. To be spontaneous means to follow the natural course. Zhuang Zi, the number two master of Taoism, beat his basin and sang when he heard of his wife's death. In defiance of common sense, he expressed his feelings in what he conceived of as the most natural: to die is natural and to celebrate it is equally natural.

In everyday life, spontaneity as Zhen or sincerity can be observed and testified to only through intersubjective activities. When your parents are getting older, Confucius once said, you feel at once happy and worried, because longevity is accompanied by senility. You cannot control your feeling, which comes naturally from the bottom of your heart. Mencius offered another illustration: a man suddenly sees a little child about to fall into a well. No matter who he may be, he will experience a feeling of horror and pity. He feels so, without thinking that he may gain the favor of the child's parents or seek the praise of his neighbors and friends. It comes from an instinctive sympathy, which is a part of the endowment of every normal human being. And that is spontaneity and sincerity, or Zhen. If the above two classical examples argue for "natural goodness" in the name of Zhen, then based on it is "moral goodness," which aims at regulating social relationships. In one's family, Zhen as sincerity is specified as filial duty. It does not amount to providing as much material comfort as possible to one's parents. Confucius once criticized this understanding, saying that it did not differ in essence from raising dogs. Filial piety is respect and love from within, paralleling the parental kindness toward children. In society, a successful interpersonal relationship also depends on sincerity for its maintenance. Confucius interpreted it as Xin (信), meaning "trust" in each other's reliability. How can trust relate to sincerity or Zhen? It could do so because trust is not necessarily secured, according to Confucius, by external conventions or legal contracts but rather is based on those moral principles that have been internalized into people's everyday behavior. But can man afford to trust himself? *The Doctrine of the Mean* gives a positive answer on the condition that one can do away with self-deception. How? Further argumentation then gives rise to the well-known Confucian proposition: "The superior man is watchful over himself when he is alone." It was so influential that Mr. Liu Shao-qi, the number two Party leader before the Cultural Revolution (1966–1976), managed to adapt it to the needs of contemporary ideology by substituting "the Party member" for "the superior man." Without an external authority like God to keep a watchful eye on him, man is alone and has to trust himself. Zhen as sincerity is his last resort.

ZHEN: THE PRESENT AND THE ULTIMATE

When Zhen means real, it refers to both actual existence and the ultimate concern without implication of transcendency toward the other world. If God is at once transcendent and immanent, the eternal Tao (Way) is immanent only. The ontological other world is unreal, the opposite of Zhen. That is why *The Doctrine of the Mean* holds: "The Tao (Way) is not far from man. When a person tries to pursue a course, which is far from the common indications of consciousness, this course cannot be considered the Tao (Way). . . . [The superior man] seeks to reach the greatness and brilliancy and also follows the path of the Mean." The present and the ultimate are interrelated and complementary. Both are Zhen (real). Zhen in the sense of actual existence adds a realistic dimension to its metaphysical nature, whereas the latter gives grounds for and makes possible the former. Of course, it does not follow that the transcendent tendency does not exist in the history of Chinese ideas. The local religion based on Taoism does talk about a world of gods. But, interesting enough is that "gods" are described as "Zhen people." On top of that, the primordial concern of Taoist monks is not the spiritual survival in the afterlife but an eternal bodily existence in this world.

Buddhism seems to have turned the real-unreal dichotomy upside down. Early Buddhism from India regards the physical world as unreal: Zhen or real is Nirvana, the final beatitude that transcends suffering, karma, and samsara. The Real demands the extinction of desire and individual consciousness and belittles the significance of the external world. But to Buddhism transformed and accepted in China, the gap between the two worlds is not that big. The doctrine about the Middle Way of the Buddha is shared by all Buddhist schools, which only differ in their interpretations. The Tian Tai School (天台宗) in China developed a peculiar interpretation: "The perfect harmony of the three levels of truth (三谛圆融)." They are called the truth of emptiness (真谛), temporary truth (俗谛), and the truth of the mean (中谛). All dharmas are empty because they have no nature of their own but depend on causes for their production. This is the truth of emptiness. On the other hand, dharmas are actually produced and do possess temporary and dependent existence. They are temporary truth. Being both empty and temporary is the nature of dharmas. This is the truth of the mean. The three involve each other or the three are one and one is three. Here we find something different from early Buddhism: though Emptiness renders dharmas really empty, dependent existence makes them relatively real. Here, the Middle Way means a synthesis of phenomenon and noumenon and a harmonization of transcendence and immanence. The balance between the present and the ultimate in terms of Zhen seems maintained at another level. An attempt to bridge the real (nirvana, beatitude, etc.) and the unreal (the mundane, the temporary, etc.) can be felt in the whole doctrine of the Tian Tai School. But it is in the Chinese Zen that the attempt achieves its final success.

Zen is the Japanese translation, pronounced Chan in Chinese, of the Sanskrit *dhyana*, meaning meditation. But meditation changed its character at the very beginning when Buddhism entered China. It was largely valorized by the Lao Zi cult prevailing at that time. As a result, meditation was and still is understood in the Taoist sense of conserving energy, reducing desire, preserving nature, and even breathing. This is something very different from the Indian concentration. Another distinction of the Chinese Zen consists in its emphasis on the enlightenment of the mind at a particular moment within this world (觉); the opposite is perplexity or confusion (迷). But this polarization in terms of mental state breaks down with ease; the doctrine argues that Buddha-mind exists in all human beings so that everyone can become Buddha so long as one persists in one's meditation. What is more significant, this assumption about human nature provides the necessary condition for what is called by some contemporary scholars "immanent transcendence"—transcending this world through one's existence in this very world. It is now generally acknowledged that Chinese meditation works with the aid of external influence, operates in this world, stresses quick wit and insight, and aims at self-realization. In other words, it aims high (the ultimate concern) but stops short at pure, exclusive transcendence (concern for the present).

Generally speaking, the ultimate concern presupposes an action that is transcendent in nature. When transcendence is conceived of as the real, spatiotemporal phenomena would fall under the unreal. It leads to the classical distinction between being and existence, intelligible and sensible, characteristic of Platonism and orthodox theology. On the contrary, Chinese intellectual culture tends to obscure the distinction by rendering this-worldness real in various ways. It results in less tension, felt and perceived by the mind, between this world and the other world, between mundane and spiritual. "Combination of Heaven and man" is another expression for the reconciliation. It is within this intellectual context that one can map out the operation of the Chinese pragmatism. To be practical entails, in the same context, the suppression of nonrational elements, thus marginalizing spiritual pursuit in the sense of religion. When the mundane or the practical carries weight, one's sense of Zhen as real corresponds to the stability of social conventions, which often play the role of anonymous authority that tells us what is real and what is unreal. Then, the integrating of the ultimate and the present into the category of Zhen might lead to a bias toward the present and cultivate a past-oriented value standard. This is the tension within the category of Zhen, persisting in all its semantic aspects.

from Europe

TRUTH IN FRANCE

———

Bertrand Ogilvie

Translated by Saroj Bhutani

WESTERN THOUGHT, EVER SINCE the birth of philosophy in ancient Greece, has made truth the pivot of its activity, to the detriment of every other undertaking. "Plato is dear to me, but truth even more so." Over and above its value as an anecdote, this remark, attributed to Aristotle, has much to teach us. By subordinating the person of Plato to the problem of truth, the philosopher discredits a whole assembly of traditional centers of authority, these being the family, relationships, friendship, as also political and religious authority, finally even intellectual authority itself. This apparently innocuous expression is actually symptomatic of a decisive turning point introduced in Greek thought around the fifth century B.C. and to which we, in the West, still subscribe.

This reversal needs to be adequately understood if we are to give full meaning to the changes that the notion of truth has undergone in the course of the centuries, up until its final contemporary convulsions, and up until the specifically social and political problems that it comes up against in the face of present-day conflicts. Numerous groups of people today in Europe, and more so in the richer countries that are a prey to the fallout of neocolonialist policies, consider truth as if it were a conviction that could be claimed as a belonging (my truth, our truth), even if this possession of a (generally religious) identity makes itself felt within an equation of power without any procedure of confrontation or of demonstration being contemplated. The path taken can be assessed in the following manner: from the truth that was a force of authority in ancient Greece, we have crossed over to truth as a demonstration, in the two separate configurations of ancient and of modern thought, finally to truth as identity. These three "moments" do not constitute as many separate and independent periods of history from the point of view of their content. At each moment, it is one of the forms of truth that is dominant without the others disappearing for all that. In the contemporary period, for example, while the organization of work and of political relationships in the industrialized countries is largely dominated by a rationalist conception of truth based on arguments or on demonstrations, it is other different paradigms of authority that govern large segments of the existence of peoples. In the context of the family or of the social background, or again in that of the fashion media and of the networks of images and sounds that give it a form, as also in that of religious practices, beliefs, and slogans, it is other criteria of truth that govern ways of behavior and lay down norms of life and thought. We see the appearance of remarkable divergences between socialized behavior and private, even intimate, behavior, which can lead to a considerable increase in psychic disorders or civil violence for example. Now, it is not possible to understand the surge of the new components of truth as an identity and to protect oneself against its more dangerous deviations except by reevaluating the scope and the limits of the face of truth around which twenty-five centuries of science and politics have been constructed.

The first claims to truth emerged in the politico-religious context of what specialists have called the "masters of truth." Truth was then linked to a supremacy, that is to say to a position of authority and of political, legal, ideological, and repressive power: the word of truth, indissolubly interpretative and normative, stating the order of the world and giving the commands that arose from it, emanated from persons (kings, priests), from whom, considering their specific situation and their superior essence or nature, it drew precisely its value. It was this linking of the truth to the person of he who pronounced it that was to be challenged by the appearance of a new type of discourse: mathematics (geometry, arithmetic), which came from Egypt and received its momentum with philosophers such as Thales. It presented a model that was indeed absolutely original in its discursive construction: a kind of *logos* entirely independent of the personality of whoever was expressing it, to be reiterated at will by any individual whatsoever and likely to produce truths that were demonstrable by themselves, without reference to, or without the backing or guarantee of, any authority external to the rules of the formation and the working of the discourse itself.

The subversive impact of mathematics did not escape the then contemporaries who immediately perceived its relationship with the new forms of political and legal organization with which the Greek city was experimenting at the time. Also, it was on the plane of equality, through argumentation and the search for demonstration, without allegiance to any authority, that public matters were being decided, in political assemblies as in the courts. Thus truth was no longer that which was stated under exceptional conditions on the basis of a revelation granted to a few privileged persons, but that which was being established from day to day through a debate and a search in which all were equals, and who could at any moment question and redefine the procedures of establishment and verification of the demonstration.

This extension of the processes of production of the truth from mathematics toward political and emotive "human affairs" has thus become one of the wagers of history and philosophy, from the time of Democritus to the present day. It was highlighted in the inexpiable struggle conducted by Plato against Democritus around the question of causality, the resumption of the Democritean program by Spinoza against Descartes with his project of dealing with passions as points, surfaces, and solids, the projects of Condorcet, of Saint-Simon, then of Auguste Comte of a "social physics" in the nineteenth century, and the structuralist reorganization of the disciplines called the human sciences or social sciences in the twentieth century. During the course of this history, which is not presented as following a linear path, even less as a progress, but rather as the repetition of a single argumentative matrix incessantly integrating from different data the notion of truth, under the effect of different "skeptical" (Montaigne) or "epistemological" (Bachelard) interventions, or of both of these (Pascal), continuously confronted by its pluralization, it became relevant to oppose "the truth" as a self-founded exclusive absolute, to "truths" as moments of a process including falsehood or error. After Spinoza, Hegel had speculatively evolved this analysis, which subsequently became classical and difficult to get around. The truth was not the simple result of a quest that could ignore its steps, its stages, and its gropings; it was the overall assembly of the process itself that remained entire, in each of its moments, the presence of truth in action, the truth of this instant and of this place, elucidation and effective explication, although transitory.

But the (provisional) relevance of the question, during the start of the twenty-first century, presents an original institutional configuration, with a wealth of social and political effects. The epistemological status of scientific production has momentarily stabilized away from the theme of a single and absolute truth, both in a negative and a positive manner: the sciences no longer seek to apprehend truth but produce truths that connect to each other and mutually absorb each other within the continuum of a symbolic-technical construction, that is to say a technological world that is embodied in the daily life of individuals and changes its very material and psychic categories. The universe of the techno-sciences is no longer an enterprise to gain knowledge of a nature whose truth it states, but the construction of a second nature whose guiding value is no longer that of what is true but of what is real, particularly of what is effective and profitable. In tandem, a strain of identity and the sense of belonging is inducted collectively and subjectively into the truth. The pluralization of the true, and in fact the disappearance of its theme within the institutional order of the techno-sciences, promotes the model of pluralization in the existential (that is to say religious, ideological, and political) order. The old "to each his truth" acquires force and a new legitimacy arising out of the joint effects of epistemological pluralization, of the disqualification of the political and social models distinct to the new postcolonial world order, and the more and more patent contradiction between the claims to democracy by the rich countries and their local (legal) and international institutions (UNO), of the structural inequality maintained, on the economic as well as political plane, within countries (poverty, citizenship at different speeds), as well as between the dominant countries and those that attempt, more or less successfully, to emerge. Thus the notion of truth is found redefined as an index of dignity and of individual (subjective or collective) existence, as a mark of singularity that may eventually adopt an aggressive line of conduct and then simply fall in line with a relationship of a struggle for power, resistance, or conquest.

TRUTH AND UNIVERSALITY

It would be wrong to see in this configuration a deviation or a historical misconstruction of the notion of truth. It is much more pertinent to perceive in it the indelible trace of the contradiction out of which this notion has arisen: in this attempt at establishing a norm, making it possible to put an end to power equations, we should ponder over whether there are not diverse interests at play in the refusal of power struggles and if they are not incompatible with each other. Unless reference is made to a transcendence that would provide at small cost for the setting up of a neutral body (the relevance of whose establishment I, for my part, do not subscribe to), an immanent analysis of the notion of truth cannot do away with the difficulty of this impure origin. It leads one inevitably to question the status of universality in which category of truth trust has been placed as much by religious monotheists of the areas surrounding the Mediterranean as by the sciences and philosophies emanating from this same region of the world. These types of universalism, incontestably, cannot equate each other to the extent to which their bases, their structures, and their procedures of construction differ considerably and are even radically opposed to each other. There is nothing in common, it seems, between the "catholicity" of the revelation, the universality of the criteria of demonstration and of experimentation, the universality of human rights and of the rights of the citizen, for which Edgar Morin had formed the suggestive neologism of "catholaïcité" (catholic-secularity).

There is nothing in common, if not precisely this form of universality, which, being stated necessarily in the situation of a singularity, opens up to a critical dialectics, which has not escaped certain philosophers. It has not escaped the attention of Machiavelli, for example, who sees in political philosophy an analysis of singular situations that cannot claim without some imposture to raise themselves to a point of view external to equations of power. In his dedication to *The Prince*, the famous metaphor of the mountain and the valley is enlightening:

> And I do not wish that one should subscribe to the presumption that a man of low and mean status should embolden himself to hold forth on and to reduce to rules, the governments of princes, because, like those who give shape to countries establish themselves in the plains in order to consider the nature of mountains and other high places, and to consider that of low places, establish themselves up above in the mountains, similarly, in order to know the nature of the people, it is necessary to be a prince and to know that of princes, it is proper to be one among the people.

It is impossible to ignore the fact that truth (in the fields of politics, philosophy, science, and religion) has always been the wager of attempts at legitimization and absolutization, which have taken the help of its imagistic and symbolic prestige to impose specific powers. And notably on the rest of the world: the conquest of the Americas, the colonization of different countries, the progressive or brutal elimination of different cultures and languages, that is to say of alternative societal and economic patterns, present-day globalization finally, only constituting just some of the most visible episodes of this history of truth and of its wagers. It should be added that it is also within this same tradition that some of the most radical criticisms and protests against this mortiferous intrication have appeared at very varied periods, as we can count among their proponents Foucault, Lévi-Strauss, Nietzsche, and Pascal, for example.

It is necessary to re-create the internal dialectics of this notion to understand the way in which its very structure lends brazenness both to its utilization as well as to a utilitarian criticism leading to the foreseeing of an incessant critical function of what is true. To quote some words borrowed from Georges Canguilhem (who in turn took them from Koyré), one could say that instead of seeking the truth, seeking to say it, to be it, to embody it and to exercise it, we would work toward wending our way "within the true," that is to say, cease to oppose the true and the false in order to highlight their permanent, inevitable interdependence: verification instead of the truth. Thus a scientific proposition may be selectively and individually false insofar as it does not allow for elucidation until the end of the process that has been its object, while being at the same time "within the true" to the extent to which it executes a pattern of research that will lead, beyond some more errors, to a pertinent result. Conversely, an apparently correct proposition that does not fall within any network of related meanings or makes it possible to pursue any further development is neither true nor "within the true."

JUDGMENT AND TRUTH

The peculiarity of Greek thought lies in its having shielded the question of truth from the immediate wagers of power or possession, and in having invented a dimension (the Greek language calls it a "topos," a place) from which some conditions of possibility of this truth can be stated: it is the question of the criteria of truth that controls in its major part the Western issue of the theories of knowledge.

In this perspective, the truth is not a thing but the possible quality of a judgment to the extent to which it makes a statement about that which is. "The true and the false are attributes of language, not things and where there is no language there is neither truth nor falsehood" (Hobbes). As Descartes points out, the very idea of a chimera is neither true nor false (it exists simply in my mind when I think of it) as long as I have not expressed a view about the real existence of such a being; that is to say, as long as I have not formed a judgment over its existence. The question, therefore, arises of the nature of this act that attempts to match a perception with a thing.

True, an important nuance makes itself felt between the position of Plato and that of Aristotle. Only the latter defines strictly, for the first time, what has been called since then the logical truth. In his *Metaphysics* and in *About Interpretation*, he reserves the legitimate use of the word truth to the qualification of declarative propositions, those that carry a meaning. The truth is in line with an alternative, which is that of the true and of the false and whose value lies only in the context of a strategy of enunciation. "Socrates is a man" is true, "Socrates is a dog" is false, but these propositions do not in any way fix the absolute, ontological value of Socrates, of man and of the dog. On the other hand, we find in Plato (and again in present-day modern language) the idea of a value of truth attributed to the very being of certain realities, contrary to others: we talk of true gold, or of true virtue as opposed to a metal or to a type of behavior that displays only the appearance of these models. On the true/false couple is superimposed that of the real and of appearance, and rather than dealing with a logical truth we are dealing with a Truth-Good having an ontological or metaphysical sweep. It is this archetypal conception of truth that enabled Christianity to find in Plato a conceptual source justifying the idea of associating the true with the divine. It is this again that we find in Hegel, in whose vocabulary the "true by itself and for itself" refers to the real in the totality of its determinations.

However, this opposition does not affect the basic orientation of the concept. Proof of this is found in the structure of the term in which it is stated right from the beginnings of philosophy. In Greek, truth is called "a-lèthéia," "that which is not hidden," or "that which is not forgotten." This negative or privative turn of phrase can suggest two interpretations, one positive and liberating, the other negative and nihilistic. The first is that of Plato: the truth is that which is known since always and which can be found anew simply through the effort of reminiscence. It is "opinion," the vitality of the senses, and the presence of the body that hinder the direct vision of essences or of ideas, models of all things and therefore the only authentic realities. Plato describes this structure of knowledge through some myths that relate the many ups and downs of the former life of souls, of their "fall" in the world ("topos") of sense realities and of bodies that are nothing but copies of the forms by themselves, and of their necessary conversion and return toward the place ("topos") or the home of intelligibility, through philosophy. In terms other than those of the fable, this pattern indicates that truth is on the side of ideas or of the intellect, not in the modern, subjective meaning of the term, but in the sense in which the intelligibility of the real is thinkable and possible only on the basis of a transcendent, objective, finalized and meaningful order (that is how Leibniz, from the Christian point of view, understood Plato).

In modern terms, we would say that in such a perspective, stress is laid on the origin of the meaning on the basis of a culture or of language, independent of any individual sense experience, which can only come second and is finally not relevant. Knowledge of the truth does not come from things or from experience; it is not encountered as a novelty, but is found in an actualization of schemas that precede and surpass the individual.

The construction of the truth is a reconstruction, a rediscovery of the meaning already there, working within the structure of the conditions of the possibilities of thought. Learning, far from being a progressive and adventurous journey, is a climb back to the sources of culture, momentarily hidden, forgotten by the individual lost in the psychic and corporal immaturity of both his real and metaphorical childhood.

We can conceive of an even more radical manner of interpreting the "a-lèthéia" of the Greeks. The truth in that case is found in a more inherent and structural manner in the unveiling not of a simple anecdotal forgetfulness, but of a constitutive veiling, of a loss inherent in the act of knowing. In this meaning, the truth would not have a simply positive content but would be doubly negative: it would consist in the unveiling of a primary dissimulation, the denunciation of a forgetfulness, the negation of a negation. This negation of the forgotten would not be a state, the condition of possibility of a knowledge, but a movement peculiar to the act itself of knowing, which, on its part, would begin by a forgetfulness. Why? Because to know is to name, and to name is to substitute realities with elements of language within which the very things fall into forgetfulness at the precise moment when they occur in the discourse. This is the way that Heidegger comments on the term *a-lèthéia*, by taking the help of a theory of language that places on the very level of enunciation the first distancing of the real, which cannot be ignored if we want an act of knowledge to take place, but for which the task of philosophy would be to recall the effects of loss. To say, or to name, means substituting the thing itself by a network of meanings that mask it and erase it in the very movement when it reveals it on the symbolic or the cultural plane. As Mallarmé has put it so well, "the flower, the absentee in every bouquet." But the discourse is also this place in which the destructive nature of the "power of elocution" can be uttered.

Without such an attempt at veracity, at an unveiling of the veiling that enunciation constitutes, the discourse could be taken to be a reality without limits, an absolute, the Absolute Itself.

Behind every attempt at enunciation of a positive truth, not including this dialectic of the "a-lèthéia," is always hidden a theologico-political enterprise, the project of a Church: thus the Gospel according to John begins by the well-known words, "In the principle was the logos, the word." But in the principle of what? Not in the principle (or, according to some translations "in the beginning") of all, or of the whole, but in the principle of this dialectical movement by which there occurs a world for usages of discourse, which, by their plurality, present the question of their comparison, of their confrontation, and of the developments and validations that they make possible and give rise to.

In one case the word is the instrument of a transparency pitted against the momentary opacity of the being. In the other, it is the very place of the opacity, for to speak or to think is first of all to cover the real with a fictional double. The truth is that which is originally turned away, buried by the first gesture that attempts to seek it, to find it, to express it. It is this that Nietzsche means when he asserts that all knowledge is an interpretation. That is also the position held by Heidegger. In both cases there is a process, an unveiling. But whereas in the case of the former it is a matter of unveiling the being by means of language, in the latter case, the very being of the language is unveiled as an original veil from below which it is not certain that one can come back.

It needs to be noted that in both cases this journey is always finalized and that the truth is immediately revealed, not as an indifferent ratio or a neutral thing, but as a value, a fundamental vector as much in the field of knowledge as in those of ethics and of politics.

THE THING IN TUNE WITH THE INTELLECT

From an initial point of view that is not primarily out of tune with common sense, the truth therefore results from an adequacy or a (direct or dialectized) conformity between the discourse that the thinking being holds on the real, and this real itself. But this device, which seems so natural, is actually the result only of long habit. What can be clearer, more indisputable in appearance than this binary vision of the act of knowing, which displays itself on the model of the reflection or of the mark? The thing is reflected in the mirror, the stylet leaves a mark in clay or on the papyrus, the world registers itself through our senses on our mind. But the physical metaphor is deceptive: it erases as if by magic the presence in the world of words and of ideas, their coefficient of reality irreducible to a simple instrumentality or to a reflection. Where there is perhaps continuity and equivalence, it invents both a duality and an asymmetry (between what reason conceives and what appears to the senses, for example). The moral desire to eliminate appearances is clearly in Plato an inauguration of the device of what in Western thought is called representation (*Vorstellung* in German). In this device, we see that the two terms are not necessarily fixed and that they can be interpreted and in a way occupied by different entities.

Thus, in a realistic perspective of the truth like that of Aristotle, then of Thomas Aquinas, what matters is the conformity between the thing and the mind (*"adaequatio rei et intellectus"*), a relationship in which reality is in the position of a criterion that does not take away from it any ontological dignity as compared to the mind. In Plato, also a realist in his own way, everything nevertheless gets reversed. The thing changes its status; it is no longer the material or empirical reality, but the reality, the only reality, of the forms or ideas that the soul must rediscover. In a way, thought is a dialogue of the soul with itself, but it is basically the conditions of the possibility of a regained conformity that philosophy is entrusted with organizing. Even with Kant, the binary structure of representation holds its own. True, it remains Platonist on the point that empirical reality is disqualified to the benefit of another transcendentalist one, that is to say, consisting in the dimension of the a priori categories of keys to reading, making it possible to detect and to decipher a world. But this other reality is that of the subject himself in his rational dimension, and he thereby acquires a constitutive function of constructor of the object of knowledge. The representation no longer describes only the relationship of the subject to the object, but it takes on the status of the object itself. The ob-ject, a constructed reality, placed, thrown before (ob) oneself is the result of this enterprise of commensuration, of adaptation of the unknowable, unapproachable (the "thing in itself") real, with the subject, through the joint play of sensibility, of understanding, and of reason, which give birth thus to a world. The knowledge of the truth is no longer the putting into operation of a representation, but it is a re-presentation, that is to say, a construction of a well-formed world as an object whose sole rational version is supplied by the science of mathematics: the world of phenomena.

Thus Kant can repeat the expression, "Truth is the conformity of thought with the object." But this assertion introduces a distinction between material truth and formal truth. On the first plane (and we are thereby leaving the circle of classical metaphysics) there cannot be a universal criterion guaranteeing the material truth of a judgment. For it is not possible to come out of the conditions of the experience that constitute the existence of the world of objects. In other words, none of our truths has the means to guarantee that it is materially adequate to the world of things such as they are, independently of us, outside the constitutive play of re-presentation. On the second plane, it is possible to describe a formal criterion that consists in conformity of judgment with the laws of thought. Philosophy does not lead to any truth by itself, but it describes the conditions for the possibility of a true discourse, that is to say, an objective one, granted to the object and therefore finally to itself. Hence the expression, "Truth is the concordance between understanding and reason," or "Truth and falsehood are found only in judgments. Truth conforms to the object when it conforms to itself." We see the subversive sweep of these theses. Truth can no longer be linked to an external body, ever likely to be transformed into a dogmatic authority, since it depends completely on the legislating activity of the rational subject. As Kant says, no truth, no idea can escape the court of reason, which alone decides on its legitimacy.

We can go a little further in this direction. If the truth results from a concordance, it can be that of the discourse with itself to the extent to which it also is a reality. The formal truth, and no longer only logical, is then that of a discourse that obeys its own rules of construction: it is said to be a true, well-formed proposition within a language whose rules of syntax have been fixed. In this sense we must admit that there exist as many concepts of truth as there are distinct systems of propositions (Carnap). This idea of truth, for internal and apparently sterile use, seems furthest from the ideal that claims to govern, in the traditional conception, the philosophic quest.

But the idea of re-presentation continues, besides, to make truth dependent on a subjective ahistorical activity, and without ties to a collectivity or to interests. In other words, this emancipation of truth remains in another way a servitude to the subjective abstract conditions of the exercise of reason. Now the idea of a god is not the only authority that claims to surpass and challenge such a criterion of re-presentation. The history of reason as a collective activity such as we see it at work in the sciences makes the same claim, and perhaps on better grounds. One will then consider, as Hegel says, that philosophy, overstepping the subjective conditions of representation, must try to allow the system of the effective presentation of the true to unfold itself in the totality of its determinations, without any subject, or any specific or transcending authority, standing in surety for it. It is history, in its immanent movement, which is then the sole judge. Material truth dealt on the contrary with the relationship with things and with facts. It could be expected to arise out of a prior agreement between thought and the world (in the Leibnizian idealism or in a providentialist religious perspective) or out of an agreement resulting from a genesis of ideas on the basis of experiences (empiricism). But we can also consider it as the result of a practical, historical, and collective process which, proceeding through incessant rectifications, pursues indefinitely the establishment of an objectivity: this is the idea of an experimental science (Claude Bernard). However, an experimental truth only finds its potential in a perpetual questioning.

At the close of this development of the idea of conformity, it is the ideal of a truth that would unite demonstration to reason, such as formulated by Descartes and grasped in an exemplary fashion in the experience of the *cogito*, which seems to be getting undone. For the sciences no longer refer to the notion of an eternal truth thought of as an absolute objectivity. This notion breaks out into a multiplicity of truths, that is to say of valid results, which are more marks of operative approaches, that is to say, that produce new results, and asymptomatic of an objectivity that is never achieved in a substantialist perspective as a thing, but only as the effective nature of a process (Bachelard). When a contemporary scientist declares that one is never as close to the real as when a scientific theory fails to take note of it, we see indeed that he no longer says "close to the true," and that he means by this that the effective structure of a phenomenon, particularly when it concerns a constructed object, appears better in a sharp denial brought to an interpretation (for one is sure then of what it is not) than in a confirmation about which one is never certain that it is not partial or even illusory (such as the madman who says "it is daytime" at high noon, a truth that is no longer one when one knows that he says this also at midnight). What indeed is an experimental confirmation, if not a setting subjected to the conditions of a guided questioning? Thus, paradoxically, a false result can be more true than a true one, for the element of truth that it enables to bring out as a horizon of questioning of new steps and new investigations has greater relevance and grasp over the real than an isolated truth about an object which often, as Bachelard says, "chooses us out more than we choose it."

THE ELEMENT OF TRUTH

This confusion of objectivity with truth rests on a conception of thought as representation, and of language as an instrument of this representation. It is perhaps not of primary importance to doubt that scientific knowledge arrives at the real. But it is more important to note that it does not arrive at it as an objectivity standing in surety for a truth. In this meaning the concept of formal truth that seemed at first sterile has the merit of linking the truth to an internal functioning, by doing away with the question of the criteria that make it possible to establish an external relationship between an idea and a thing. For, as Spinoza has written, an idea is "something real," and in this respect it cannot be opposed to things, since, far from representing them, it is part of them. A false idea does not represent a thing badly; it is incomplete in the very order of ideas. In fact, the process of knowledge deals only with more or less complete ideas, that is to say, it is more or less associated with ideas that explain them or that take account of them, and not with real ideas that never present themselves to reason other than as ideas in the element of thought or of language. "It is in this concept alone that the truth finds the element of its existence," and "The word gives to thought its highest and truest existence," writes Hegel.

We know that a fact is never given but constructed, that no immediate intuition of a fact can produce a knowledge, which is, on the contrary, as Bachelard has said, the result of the negation not so much of sense impressions as of interpretations that are too imaginative, that are never anything but representations. Hence, truth is not the relationship finally established with a reality such as it would be in itself. It is more the discovery that such a contact is impossible because there is no cause for it to be so. For thought is already entirely within the real of which it forms a part, without ever being able to grasp it as such, by giving it to oneself in the form of an interiorized confrontation between a subject and an object. If thought is part of the real, in the field of truth, in the element of language outside which the real is denied to it, the truth is still always there, but in the form of the demonstration of an original constitutive veil below which there is nothing to grasp.

One can consider two attempts at a critical challenge to representative thought, which has been until the twentieth century the natural field for anthropological reflection. The first, found in Gerard Lebrun, for example, in *la patience du concept* (the patience of the concept), undertakes, in both a Hegelian and Nietzschean tradition, to free conceptuality from every "human, too human" configuration, as Nietzsche has said. On the basis of the acknowledged finding that the immediate interest of thought leads it to find itself everywhere as if it were at home (the systems of the philosophers themselves do not escape this prevailing conformism), it becomes a matter of detecting in the history of sciences the moments of crises and of reversals when the very categories that enabled them to express themselves until then are challenged, and to confront these novel, unheard of results, which acquire a status of truth on the basis of their strangeness, of the clash and the effective transformations that they are likely to produce in reality, such as revolutions, political ones like that of 1789 in France, and theoretical ones, which radically change the data of an entire world. Evoking this incessant march of objective rationality and of its mutations, Hegel writes:

> The mind in the state of formation matures slowly and silently till its new face disintegrates fragment by fragment the edifice of its previous world; the tottering of this world is only indicated by sporadic symptoms; the frivolity and boredom which invade what still subsists, the vague premonition of an unknown are the signs which herald the fact that something else is progressing. This continuous crumbling which did not change the physiognomy at all is suddenly interrupted by the rising sun which, in an instant, outlines at one stroke the shape of the new world. [Hegel 1910, n.p.]

We see to what extent, in the history of these successive sunrises, we have given up the fixed and unchanging structure of the sun of Good, which dominates the Platonist cavern. The truth here is the complex result of the profound fermentation that animates an era without the knowledge even of its agents, but whose status arises out of its belonging to the infinite series of such momentary configurations. The truth is always truth-of (truth of a time, a situation, a conjunction of circumstances). But it can only sustain its status by integrating itself and therefore by abolishing itself in the series of other conjunctions of circumstances, which sketch out the infinite history of its accomplishment. Rarely has a less anthropomorphic and less dogmatic conception of truth been offered.

The other perspective is the one, Nietzschean also but profoundly anti-Hegelian, at least in appearance, of Deleuze (*Différence et répétition*). In an explicitly empirical perspective, it consists of seeing in concepts the object of a meeting, that is to say, the imperative prompting emanating from the things themselves; "but things in the free and wild state, beyond *anthropological predicates*," which deliver them to us preinterpreted. To confront oneself with these "always new, otherwise distributed *here and nows*" is to give oneself the means to place at a distance this picture of thought in which Deleuze sees three meanings: (1) a normative and exacting presupposition; (2) the form of the representation, a thought through subjective picturization and not through an objective concept; and (3) the discourse of the representative that is talking in our place. In other words, it is as much a matter of a thought through picturization as a thought that would unfold already on the basis of a certain picture of what it should be, of a certain presupposition concerning the thought, its speed, its urgency, its rectitude, its intentionality (in the line of Nietzschean reflection, a moral intention, a plan of life). Even more, it is a matter of a perspective on which Deleuze does not lay stress even though he clearly brings it up; the representative thought is also a thought in which the subject who thinks allows himself to represent through this general intentional presupposition known as common sense, the natural light, the desire to know, and the overall orientation toward the true and the good, whose exacting power is well known. This is a political perspective; it deals with the crucial question of the value of representativeness both in the field of collective will and in that of the (subjective) will of truth. We thus see how the space of the re-presentation characteristic of a certain component of Western thought unfolds in different directions connected to each other. It is a space that is simultaneously perspective (the vision of a world "in perspective" grasped geometrically from the point of view of a subject such as the aesthetic version of Renaissance paintings), perceptive, cognitive, and rational (the Kantian philosophy being its most accomplished version), as also political.

These two works seek, each in its way, a theory of thought without a picture, which makes the truth no longer the result of an external judgment but of a situated activity. Over and above their differences, perhaps their dissension, in both cases there is an attempt at pursuing the same task. This expression of thought without picturization is not only to be understood in the meaning of a criticism of representation. Although Nietzsche has been one of the main representatives of the criticism of this dimension, he is far from being the only one. The most original formulation is the one found in the seventeenth century in Pascal.

THE "REASON OF EFFECTS" AND THE "THOUGHT AT THE BACK"

Such a structure of the truth, formed out of the complex connection of different levels and in which the appearance is never dissociable from the truth, requires a specific form of thought. This new procedure concerns not only the science of nature but also, and above all, politics and religion. In a general reflection on illusion and therefore on the relationships between the true and the false, Pascal substitutes to the classical (Cartesian for instance) idea of truth, that of the "reason of effects," which prevents one from thinking separately of the true and the false, and includes in the definition of truth the indissociable presence of error. By "effects" Pascal means the assembly of phenomena insofar as they appear as data. Opinions, discourses, and types of behavior of individuals do not fall from the sky. They obey a pattern, they have causes (the reasons of effects), even if they appear completely illogical, absurd, and contradictory. The very existence of the contradiction between opinions or behaviors is the sign of a simple superficial putting into relationship of terms that lead fatally to preference being given to some relationships to the detriment of others, which amounts to reserving rationality only to coherence and excluding a part of the real. Some effects are seen as not being relevant as they display a disturbance of will or of freedom that cannot be theorized. This way of thinking is, for Pascal, inadequate. The necessity of taking account of the contradiction itself leads to the idea that there is a logic of the absurd, of incoherence, and that it should be uncovered if we wish to understand the working of the world both in its actions as in its words. True causality, therefore, can fall only into another rank, not in the sense of a transcendence, but in the sense of a hidden, invisible reason of structure. Abandoning all surface thought, "outside" thought, which is satisfied with denouncing the illusions of others to make them an object of derision, Pascal suggests that we make use of the "thought from behind," a process of elucidation which, going beyond appearances, progresses to the point of bringing out in return their basis, succeeds in getting them understood both as such and as founded, as effects and as reasons. To think true, therefore, is to bring out the meaning of the false, for the true is never anything but the completely evolved meaning of the false. This idea is fraught with consequences, since it leads to the discovery that every truth has itself a meaning, which is also, in a certain way, a falsehood full of meaning:

> We should have a thought at the back and judge everything by that, while speaking however like the people. . . . It is therefore correct to say that everyone is in a state of illusion, for even though the opinions of the people are healthy, they are not so in their heads, for they think that the truth lies where it is not. The truth

is indeed in their opinions, but not to the extent that they imagine. It is true that gentlemen should be honoured but not because birth is an effective advantage, etc. Opinion of healthy people. The greatest evil is civil war. [Pascal 1909–1914, n.p.]

It needs to be noted that the reasoning we are dealing with is very close to that of Freud; it is the very structure of the dream or of the symptom to think and to present precisely the truth, there where it is not. The interpretative method that Pascal calls the "thought at the back" takes on a meaning with relation to other modes of thought from which it is distinguished. The first, which Pascal calls "opinion of the people," consists in a belief, that is to say, in an immediate adherence to an appearance. It is therefore not a matter of a sociological category but of a mode of consciousness, or even a degree of knowledge. The people honor great persons because their birth confers on them a nature superior to that of others, and their clothes, the marks of respect that surround them, are the expression of this eminence. The great persons themselves are a part of the people, the aristocrats as much as the sociological people, and even more insofar as they are obviously the first to believe in their own superiority. The skeptics, on the contrary, the rationalists, the libertines, future philosophers of the Enlightenment, see in these opinions errors, illusions ("They are men like us"), and think they have arrived at a truth by denouncing these false qualities as conventional, based solely on custom and forgetfulness of the origin. Pascal calls this second mode of consciousness, which is totally summed up in a denunciation, that of the "half clever" or the "philosophers." This corresponds in Spinoza to he who would say, "We are not free," as against the people for whom "We are free" is said without any of them understanding that I believe I am free because I am unconscious of the causes that determine me, and that there is in this erroneous belief a sort of necessity.

It is a narrow, limited rationalism, which expresses truths without seeing the relationship that links the truth to error, and which makes out truth to be like a justification for the existence of the error. The philosopher is he who speaks as if he had no body, no position, no place; it is he who excludes himself from what he says, who talks of the (immense and distant) sun as if he does not see it from a point of view (from where he appears necessarily small and close by), and who thinks an abstract objectivity independent of all subjectivity. He is Descartes, for example.

To have the "thought at the back" is, on the contrary, to accede to this third mode of knowledge, which Pascal calls that of the "clever ones," which makes it possible to understand that social hierarchy has a meaning, a function—that of keeping the human community in a viable form (sheltered from civil war, "which is the worst of evils")—and that the first mode of knowledge, the opinions of the people, plays a cementing role in this hierarchy, which makes them necessary, healthy, and therefore in their own way true, but not for the reasons that the people believe. The "clever one" is not a hypocrite; he does not say anything other than what he thinks. He is the one who succeeds in thinking of two things at the same time, illusion and its necessity; he talks like the people while judging from his "thought at the back." He submits himself, he bows down, knowing full well why he is right in doing so. For it is this network of illusions and conventions that goes into the making of the world, making it function, through which he finds his legitimacy. This legitimacy that reveals the thought at the back has obviously nothing absolute about it. It does not have a basis by right. It is, on the contrary, completely factual and relative. Not undetermined or undeterminable, but linked to some conditions of a determined functioning. It appears, therefore, once again that the specific order of the custom, of the social structure, is not a community offered for the accomplishment of a sovereign good, but a political field grasped in a state of balance, of stability, in accordance with immanent norms. The truth, in politics as elsewhere, is not simply relative, it is relative to; it expresses the conditions on the basis of which a conjunction of circumstances is made authentically possible, viable, durable, and effective.

The "thought at the back" is much more than a simple method of knowledge. Through it there already appears the idea of the Hegelian dialectics; indeed, if the thought at the back brings to our knowledge the structures of the visible, it is because the real itself is infinite and contradictory, and even more so because the thought at the back is itself a part of the reality. The structure and the movement of the real, which consist of a perpetually displaced relationship between the finite and the infinite, do not give to the thought at the back any final eminence, any status of perfect knowledge; they fit, on the contrary, into this dialectic:

> The people honour persons of high birth, the half-clever despise them, saying that birth is not a gain of the person but of chance. The clever honour them, not in the way of thinking of the people, but through the thought at the back. Pious people who have greater zeal than knowledge despise them despite this consideration which makes them honoured by the clever ones, because they judge them through the new light that piety gives them, but perfect Christians honour them by way of another higher light. This is the way successive opinions work for or against depending on the light that one has. [Pascal 1909–1914, n.p.]

This passage makes us understand that the thought at the back is not found, strictly speaking, at any fixed point in this succession of opinions; it is the series without beginning or end of the ideas that we conjure up on things according to the point of view in which we are placed. And neither is error one of them, but only the will to consider one single one as final and exclusive, which also means that all truth asserted as such and frozen in its identity, is an error. That does not mean that there are no things that are certain, but they are not those that the people believe.

THE VALUE OF TRUTH

"We have an idea of the truth, invincible against any Pyrrhonism" (Pascal). True, the modern criticism of truth is not skeptical; it does not destroy it but *situates* it, like a constitutive illusion specific to reason, to its normal functioning. If "we do indeed have a true idea" (Spinoza), that is to say, if knowledge propels itself in an element that dispenses it from seeking criteria and bases, if the course of its development unfolds independently of any normative appreciation that would seek to fit it into a hypothetical journeying toward the truth, we must nevertheless question this idea of the truth that Pascal talks of, invincible, which is not satisfied with the results that are effective but not true of scientific knowledge.

Not grasped either in the effectiveness of its results but by its presence alone, knowledge appears as an activity distinct to the life of man through which he enters into a certain original relationship with an environment. This type of relationship, moreover, is not universal, as not all peoples in every era have practiced it in the way of a search for truth in the sense of a universal value, universally communicable and operational. In this sense, truth is the specific orientation given to a search for the "direct or indirect solution of the tensions between man and his environment," which does not seek only to regain a security (Canguilhem), but attempts to give to the latter the form of a model that can be imposed on all in the name of an intrinsic legitimacy. "The truth is this kind of error without which a determined species of living beings could not live. In the final analysis, it is the value of life that is decisive" (Nietzsche). The "will for truth" would then prolong itself in terms of a valorization open to analysis within the framework of a policy. The truth would no longer be only the name of the illusion of a fixed relationship with the world (Nietzsche), but that of a finality of reason of which one would expect to be able to trace beyond the norms of a science the principles of a power.

Georges Bataille writes magnificently, "I live from sense experiences and not from logical explanations," echoing without knowing it the famous and provocative title of the opuscule of Husserl, "*La terre ne se meut pas*" (the earth does not propel itself), written at the same time, at the start of World War II. Was this a return from this side of Galilee? Not at all. It was rather meant to bring out the difficult articulation of "the human experience and of physical causality" to borrow the famous title of a work by Brunschvicg. The space in which we live is not that of a planet wandering in the infinite void, but that of "the earth, the original ark" (Husserl), a closed and fixed environment, scene of the sufferings and joys that we experience and maintain as political animals. Pluralization, or as Merleau-Ponty has said so well, "the enlargement" of reason, seems indeed to be the absolute condition of the definition of a multiple system of the truth, which transports analogically its norms over the length of diverse practices, without giving preference to any but without forgetting any either.

Although the sciences have definitely demonstrated their aptitude to define and to implement norms in the modification of nature and in the construction of a world (that of the technosciences), the principles of the organization of the relationships and the powers of the truths of one and another and of their confrontation have yet to come. What one could call the search, in politics, of a disjunctive truth that succeeds in articulating differences, not in the form of their separation and of their substantialization, but on the contrary in a dynamic enabling them to distance themselves incessantly from themselves without a preestablished finality, in the search for a vital value that would no longer be a truth but a process of uninterrupted verification, has not until now been the subject of innovative attempts. In this field, except for some extremely complex and sophisticated findings due to civilizations that have now disappeared, it is the repetition of some classical, inferior, simplistic, and brutal forms that is the rule (both in the field of political regimes and in that of matrimonial regimes, but in this latter field some novelties seem to have appeared). For long the truth has been confused with identity. It is not appropriate to situate it at present on the side of difference, but rather on the side of the possibility for every being and for every thing to differ incessantly in its difference.

WORKS CITED

Hegel, G. W. F. (1910). *The Phenomenology of the Mind*, tr. J. B. Baillie. London: George Allen Ltd.

Macchiavelli, Niccolo. (1988). *The Prince*. Cambridge: Cambridge University Press.

Pascal, B. (1909–1914). *Thoughts*, tr. W. F. Trotter. In *The Harvard Classics, Vol. XLVIII, Part 1*. New York: P. F. Collier and Son.

from India

TRUTH IN INDIAN TRADITIONS

———

Ganesh Devy

"ONCE, LONG AGO, VAJASRAVAS gave away his possessions to gain religious merit." This is how the Katha Upanishad opens. It goes on to tell us the amazing story of Vajasravas's son, Nachiketa, who appeals to his generous father to give him away to Yama, the king of death. On reaching Yama's abode, Nachiketa has to wait for three days before Yama returns home. Yama regrets that Nachiketa had to wait for three days; as an atonement for the three inhospitable nights, he grants Nachiketa three boons. "Ask," Yama says, "one for each night." "O king of death, as the first of these boons, grant that my father's anger be appeased, so he may recognize me when I return and receive me with love." For the second boon, Nachiketa asks to learn the special sacrifice-ritual that will help him to ascend to heaven. Not only does Yama teach him the fire sacrifice, but, pleased with young Nachiketa's devotion, he also pronounces that the ritual would be named after Nachiketa. "Thus have I granted you the second boon, Nachiketa, the secret of the fire that leads to heaven. It will have your name. Ask now, Nachiketa, for the third boon." Nachiketa's third prayer is to know the truth about existence. "When a person dies, there arises this doubt. 'He still exists,' say some. 'He does not,' say others. I want you to teach me the truth. This is my third boon." But this quest for truth cannot be easily fulfilled by Yama. He promises every material and celestial glory to Nachiketa in order to dissuade him from the dangerous quest. Nachiketa, however, is steadfast in his quest. "Teach me of that you see as beyond right and wrong, cause and effect, past and future," he insists.

What follows in the Katha Upanishad is probably the quintessential philosophy of life developed in ancient India. It proposed that truth, *Satya*, is beyond all attributes. It is *nirguna*, not limited by qualities, but supports all qualities, the basis of all attributes. It causes all *vikaras*, all possibilities of conceptualization, all *gunas*, the perceptible manifestations of the phenomena. But the ultimate, which has no cause, is beyond cognition, description, and verbal articulation. That can never be represented in the realm of gods, men, or demons.

The Isha Upanishad, in another statement of the all-pervasive truth that forms the permanent substratum of existence, begins with the following lines, which have been echoed innumerable times during the last three millennia in every section of India's composite social fabric:

All this is full. All that is full.
From fullness, fullness comes.
When Fullness is taken from fullness,
Fullness still remains.

The term for fullness used in the Upanishad is *purnam*. But there is no hint of perfection in that term as opposed to any kind of imperfection. From the earliest times, thinkers in India have avoided positing a binary view of truth as something that is opposed to untruth and exclusive of such an antithetical entity.

Therefore, truth, or that nameless That, *tat* in Sanskrit, also said to be Brahman, is considered the cause of the entire existence with all its past, present, and future, but That itself is not confined to any single aspect of existence. At the same time, to emphasize its all-pervasive presence, it is also said to be *tvam*, yourself, or the self in a person. Thus, in ancient India, truth was understood in terms of both the phenomenal existence and the ego field, the two seen as being truly inseparable. The most celebrated of the Upanishadic premises was *Tat Tvam Asi* (That Is You). Hence, *self* and *truth* often occur in mutually interchangeable contexts in all Upanishads.

The ancient Indian vision of life and existence has left very deep marks on every aspect of culture and has influenced the life of people in the subcontinent in every epoch of history. The attitude to truth as the dynamic process of mutual discovery between reality and self has made Indian society open to receiving cultural influences and racial influxes so as to synthesize them with Indian traditions and society. Had India not developed this great spirit of openness, the Indian civilization could not have accommodated the amazing range of theological doctrines in its cultural fold and the large waves of racial migration in its social life. Probably no other civilization has received so much from outside and has yet managed to retain its essential character as India has throughout its history.

Another important impact of the ancient Indian vision of truth was on the manner in which knowledge was cultivated in India. Search for truth has been, anywhere else in the world, the primary aim of developing various fields of knowledge. Whether it is measuring, counting, transacting, communicating, remembering, analyzing, or identifying the phenomena and objects encountered by the senses as the motive behind constructing a given field of knowledge, or whether it is imaging, depicting, abstracting, and classifying, it has always been done in other cultures in order to discover, identify, reveal, and describe truth. In these processes, the knower and that which is to be known are seen as being distinct, and the act of knowing becomes possible when the two establish a verifiable point of contact. The duality between the one who knows and that which is known was ruled out in ancient Indian thought.

The Bhagwad Gita, which presents the Upanishadic thought in an integrated and simplified version states,

> I am seated in the hearts of all. From me are memory, knowledge and their loss. I alone am the object to be known through all the Vedas; I am also the originator of the Vedanta, and I myself am the knower of the Vedas. [15:15]

Therefore, there is no privileged space for the interpreter, the scientist, and the skeptic questioner. Truth, in this version, is not just a discovery or a revelation; it takes in its fold all doubts, questions, and ecstasies. It precedes the discovering consciousness. Knowledge in this sense is to know what one already knows. It is not to be formed through continuous questioning; it has to be recollected by allowing one's memory to forget questioning. This attitude implies that knowledge gathered through sensory perception does not lead to the understanding of truth. In any case that is not knowledge but only a semblance of knowledge, a delusion. The Gita states:

> Persons who are diversely deluded do not see it [the truth] even when it is residing in this body, or experiencing, or in association with qualities. Those with the eye of knowledge see. [15:10]

The "eye of knowledge," *jnanachakshu*, is not the physical or the mental inward eye. It is not imagination, intuition, memory, or any other mental faculty. It is the ability to dissolve the self in the eternal That. The visionary eye allows one's consciousness to see that truth is the permanent and indivisible substratum of all reality, that *satya* is the basis of *sat*, truth, the pivot of all reality perceived by the senses. The senses can perceive only that which is reality; the self can see truth. Therefore, the fields of knowledge related to mapping out reality are all *vidyas*, the ones that can be learned; but the field of knowledge related to truth alone is *jnana*, a total understanding that will dissolve the duality between the knower and that which is known. Truth cannot be learned. It cannot be taught. *Vidyas* can be learned and taught. They are the disciplines charted out in terms of the sensory ability to perceive the manifest and material world. Knowledge cannot be taught or learned. It comes with the vision of the world as a deceptive layer of the phenomenal reality on top of the substratum of truth. As the Gita states:

> Of the unreal there is no being; the real has no non-existence. But the nature of both these indeed, has been realized by the seers of truth. [2:16]

Given this assertion of truth's inherent superiority over reality, of vision over learning, it was but natural that while systems of apprenticeships for material and medical sciences, political and social controls, techniques of war and love were developed and came to be respected, a special place of privilege was reserved for the seer's ability to envision. Therefore, the art of control over the mind, the science of eliminating attachments, which would initiate the subject consciousness into the vision of the unity of beings and things, came to acquire the highest cultural significance. The *rishi*, the seer, and not the thinker or the scholar, came to be regarded as the votary of truth.

In the course of time the simple verses of the Vedas, developed in folk and oral traditions of communities as yet coming to terms with their sense of wonderment about the creation and nature's variety, were given the status of sacred utterances, the god-spell. The Vedas that kept developing as a body of songs over a long period of a millennium contained verses such as these, for instance:

Who formed the heels of man?
Who formed his flesh, his ankles?
Who his well-formed fingers?
Who opened up his apertures?
Who formed the testicles in his middle part?
Who gave him a firm basis?

This verse from the Atharva-veda (X:II) views in admiration the entire process of creation without ever overlooking the physical aspect of the process. The Upanishads changed this tone of wonder and brought in the sense of a deep and philosophical mystery by positing brahman as the essential truth of existence. The inward looking Upanishadic thought privileged the meditative rishi over the Vedic hunter, king, adventurer, poet, and the wise man. Though that never can be said to be the intention of the Upanishads, the concept of truth in it became, centuries later, the cornerstone of Brahmanism in the social hierarchy and the caste and gender discrimination in education in India. The history of the rise of caste as a marker of social status has been complex and guided by numerous material conditions and historical shifts, and as such to place too much responsibility for its rise on the Upanishadic notion of truth would be inappropriate. However, that this notion as well as the understanding of other scriptures guided by it had a major share in its philosophical makeup cannot be contested.

Presenting the history of ideas in India in proper chronological order is a despairing task, and one cannot be sure if the rise of the Mahabharata in its earliest form as a chronicle of an epoch-making war predates the formulation of the Upanishads, or if the two were being developed side by side. The mere incorporation of the Bhagwad Gita, a digest of Upanishadic thought, in the Mahabharata provides no conclusive proof with regard to the chronological order. But if one overlooks such problems, and examines the Mahabharata in its own terms, one finds that already the purity of clan is a major issue in it, and the commitment to upholding this purity by using all *vidyas*, the skills related to controlling the material world, is considered the most laudable goal of life in it. Dharma is the key concept in the great epic, just as brahman is in the Upanishads.

The epic narrates a story of a war between the Pandava princes and the Kaurava princes. The Pandava princes, guided by Lord Krishna, are fighting on the side of dharma, and in fact the war itself is described as the dharma war. The virtue of the Pandavas is that they are not fighting the war out of any attachment to power and wealth but just to set right the imbalance in justice. The oldest among them, Yudhisthira, is also known as Dharmaraja, the dharma prince. He is shown as the most truthful of all princes and warriors, and possessing of wisdom closely reminiscent of Nachiketa of the Katha Upanishad. He tells a half-truth but only once, when one of his adversaries inquires, "Is it true that my son Ashwatthama is killed in the action?" Dharmaraja replies, "Ashwatthama died, but who knows whether the elephant with that name or your son." "Whether man or elephant" is an idiom that almost every modern Indian language has inherited from this infamous utterance of Yudhisthira to indicate ambivalence or a half-truth.

If the Upanishadic thinker, lost in his deep meditation and in tune with brahman, provided in later centuries the prototype for the brahman class, the great warriors of the Mahabharata, ready to lay down their lives for the upkeep of dharma, provided the prototype for the Kshatriya, the warrior class. Brahman and dharma, these two notions of truth, have sunk very deep in the soul of Indian culture and have kept surfacing in innumerable manifestations at every turn of the cultural history without the barriers of language and caste.

In the millennium preceding the Christian era, the rise of the brahmin, or the men of learning, as well as the Kshatriya, or the men of governance, had created another segment that was neither. What could be truth for it? Those belonging to this class neither had the access to brahman, the greater self, and the language in which its greatness was described, namely, Sanskrit, nor did they have much to do with dharma, being engaged in agriculture and such other productive activities rooted in the soil. Therefore, a new version of truth, an altogether new and powerful philosophy of life, sprang up in India six centuries before Christ through the teachings of Gautama, the Buddha. It said, and said so in people's language, Prakrit, that a notion of god or brahman was not necessary for the discovery of truth. No scriptures were necessary for knowing what truthfulness is. A surrender to truth itself is a surrender to dharma, and all acts of virtue have to be performed in the interest of the here and now.

As Vivekananda, a twentieth-century Indian thinker engaged in reviving the basic tenets of ancient Indian thoughts, puts it:

> This teacher wanted to make truth shine as truth. No softening, no compromise, no pandering to the priests, the powerful, the kings. No bowing before superstitious traditions, however hoary; no respect for forms and books just because they came down from the distant past. He rejected all scriptures, all forms of religious practice. Even the very language, Sanskrit, in which religion had been traditionally taught in India, he rejected, so that

his followers would not have any chance to imbibe the superstitions which were associated with it. [*Complete Works*, 1947, p. 100]

The Upanishads had taught India to efface the world of the senses. Gautama taught India to face it. When encountered by an old woman who had lost her young son, Gautama told her, "Go, and find someone whose family has not experienced death at one or another time." Death and pain must be accepted as a reality of life, for the reality surrounding us is no illusion. Truth, in Gautama's philosophy, was not the substratum of the phenomenal world; it was each and every aspect of the manifest and sensory life. Attachment to the worldly pleasures has to be contained, not because those pleasures are unreal and illusory but because pleasure and pain are so palpably real that pain and grief can be contained only if pleasure can be contained. Buddha's version of truth, too, has been as central a feature of Indian civilization as that of the Upanishads and the Mahabharata. Though Buddhism declined in India after holding sway for nearly half a millennium owing to political persecution of Buddha's followers, his teachings have remained ingrained in the popular thought and lore.

The play *Mrichhakatikam* (The Toy Clay Cart) by Shudraka, probably written in the second century, shows the political conflict between the followers of Buddha and the followers of the Sanatan dharma, the traditional vedic faith. In it, Vasantsena, a courtesan, is in love with an impoverished but generous brahman, Charudatta. Her ornaments, left in the custody of the hero, are stolen by a forest dweller, who is preparing for an armed revolution. Charudatta takes away his wife's jewelry to compensate Vasantsena. Here the untruth begins. But in the end the truth of the matter is found out. Charudatta's untruth is seen as the sign of his great love for Vasantsena. Pleasure of love, in this play, is considered as important as the primacy of truth.

Indian thinkers were aware that the question of a lie is as important as the question of truth. They tackled this question through a series of theoretical texts on poetics beginning with Bharatamuni's *Natyashastra*, composed in the second century, which has been pivotal to the Indian tradition of poetics, to Jagannatha's *Rasagangadhara*, composed in the seventeenth century. Truth has the dignity of being divine in origin. Should then fiction, which is a structured lie, be considered demonic in nature? Natyashastra had to grapple with this question. Bharata maintained that the dramatic action causes various aesthetic emotions such as anger, joy, horror, and love in the mind of the audience. These he described with the term *rasas*. A dramatic performance is expected to create the *rasas*, so as to give the audience a sense of delight, *Ananda*. Bharata maintained that the aesthetic delight had the same source as the spiritual ecstasy. His expression for this shared parentage of truth and the fictional truth is *brahmanand sahodar*: the joy in experiencing a structured work of dramatic illusion is born in the same source as the discovery of brahman as the substratum of existence. Hence, *natya*—drama—too has the status of a *shastra*, the realization of truth. Natyashastra too was given the status of a Veda in ancient India, and the creation of *rasa* came to be considered desirable as a means of realization of the brahman.

Bharata's two most eminent successors, Anandavardhana of the eighth century and Abhinavagupta of the tenth to eleventh century, continued his pursuit and further explored how words, with all their material attributes, could lead to a meaning that is pure and transcendent like the brahman. Anandavardhana's view was that the material body of language, the *Shabda*, is inherently capable of suggesting a meaning not restricted by any materiality. This is achieved by language by virtue of its structure that causes a *sphota*, a revelation of *dhvani*, the suggested meaning. Abhinavagupta emphasized the quality of aesthetic experience that dissolves fragmented human perception and creates a state of mind conducive to higher spiritual realization.

Bharata had not set the *rasas* in any hierarchy. For him, all types of aesthetic sentiment were of equal importance, but Abhinava introduced the notion that *Shanta* was the ultimate among the *rasas*. *Shanta*, the tranquil, goes beyond all dualities, beyond right and wrong, manifest and transcendent, and presents an equipoise that will bring the experience of brahman to bear upon the fictional world of poetry and drama. Thus, Indian thinkers in the field of aesthetics maintained that truth has no opposite with its own autonomous realm of existence. There is no possibility of a permanent and absolute untruth that has an existence outside the realm of brahman or truth. This assumption had serious implications for Indian civilization in the area of social ethics.

If truth has no absolute antithesis, it follows that human action cannot be divided between good and evil, between truthful and untruthful. At best it can be divided between the one that reflects the realization of truth and the one that does not. One can only say that a person is a realized one or an ignorant one. The ignorant, therefore, cannot be condemned forever as the agent of evil. Since brahman is all-pervasive, it must dawn upon the ignorant one, too, some day. The absence of a sharply defined concept of evil in Indian thought is a major distinguishing feature of Indian culture. Acceptance of these views made Indian civilization more accentuated in the direction of aesthetics than that of ethics. As a result, the religious thought in ancient India rarely attempted defining a common ethical code for all social classes. There were treatises on what the ethics of a king or the ethics of the teacher class should be. But there was no common code of ethics binding on all varnas, all sections of society. Even if the values such as generosity, compassion, and self-control were posited by the scriptures as generally desirable values of human life, an aberration from these, too, was explained away as *apad dharma*, action in a difficult situation. Probably what comes closest to the statement of an ethical code in the Indian tradition is a section from the Brihad Aranyak Upanishad (5:2).

The children of Prajapati, the Creator-gods, human beings, and *asuras*, the godless, lived with their father as students. When they had completed the allotted period the gods said, "Venerable One, please teach us." Prajapati answered with one syllable: "*Da*."

"Have you understood?" he asked.

"Yes," they said. "You have told us *damyata*, be self-controlled."

"You have understood," he said.

Then the human beings approached.

"Venerable One, please teach us."

Prajapati answered with one syllable: "*Da*."

"Have you understood?" he asked.

"Yes," they said. "You have told us *datta*, give."

"You have understood," he said.

Then the godless approached. "Venerable One, please teach us."

Prajapati answered with the same syllable: "*Da*."

"Have you understood?" he asked.

"Yes," they said. "You have told us *dayadhvam*, be compassionate."

"You have understood," he said.

The heavenly voice of the thunder repeats this teaching. *Da-da-da!* Be self-controlled! Give! Be compassionate!

The monosyllabic pronouncements of Prajapati, charged with ambivalence and open to diverse interpretations, are indicative of India's attitude to ethics. The only law in it is that whereas truth is all-pervasive, each one will understand it according to one's own *pragna*, the visionary intelligence. No interpretation of that all-pervasive presence is superior to any other interpretation. No understanding is wrong or right. The aim of every interpretation is to end interpretations; the aim of thought is to attain a total dissolution of thought. *Shanti*, the peace that passes all understanding, is the highest understanding. It is through this concept of *shanta*, leading to *shanti*, that the aesthetics of Abhinava approximated the spirituality of the Upanishads.

Because no understating of truth was to be considered imperfect in a logical, theological, or ethical sense, the Indian literary tradition did not find it necessary to develop tragedy as a form of drama. Tragedy, as developed in the Greek tradition, required the possibility of an absolute ending. Within the framework of a unified action taking place in a unit of time, the protagonist of tragedy had to overcome the flaw in his character. Fate and chance intervened to arrest the resolution of the hero's crisis, and the recognition of his condition of arrest within time and space led to the tragic ending. This kind of a structure could not have been possible in the Indian tradition owing to the denial of all absolutes other than truth or brahman. It is not limited by time or space. Hence, the idea of a unity of action defined within a unit of time and a unit of space can but be the failure of recognition of the brahman. In place of tragedy, Indian aesthetics conceptualized *karuna*, or that which moves the audience, as an aesthetic category. But *karuna*, too, ultimately leads to the realization of *ananda*, the ecstasy in the discovery of brahman. The commentators on Indian literary tradition, therefore, held that the dominant *rasa* in the Mahabharata is *shanta*, and that in the Ramayana is *karuna*.

Another consequence of positing the notion of truth as the permanent substratum of existence was the rise of belief in rebirth. If brahman is present in every animate being and inanimate object, death cannot be the absolute end of life. If recognition of the greater self by the individual self is a continuous and dynamic cosmic process, then there arises the need to have a possibility of existence beyond death. If all beings are equal manifestations of brahman, rebirth need not bring the member of a species back to the same species. Rebirth, therefore, came to be an essential component of Indian thought, except in the schools, which denied the existence of brahman altogether.

The tremendous freedom and excitement provided to imagination by the notion of rebirth enriched Indian literature in every form, theological as well as secular. It influenced the significance attached to familial relationships and the structure of the society stratified into *varnas*. It opened up the possibility of conceptualizing the rebirth of gods as *avataras*, and the theological potential of positing hundreds of different godheads to represent the great variety of nature's creation.

It would be wrong to assume that the purely aesthetic notion of life is based on the view that the discovery of brahman is the ultimate source of delight, and that the search for causal relationships in human time is a futile exercise born out of *avidya*, ignorance or a lapse of memory, which never received refutations and challenges. Kumarila Bhatta, for instance, argued from the standpoint of the mimansa school of thought that to take brahman as a certainty in the absence of any proof of its verifiable perception would be absurd. "If nobody saw God before He created the universe, how can we assert that He is the cause?" was his question.

The question of the beginning is as important in the formation of notions of truth as the question of the ending of the universe. The mimansa school of Kumarila and its contemporary grammarian school led by Bhartrihari took up these issues and generated a profound philosophical debate about the verbal texture of truth and its perception. Bhartrihari himself was the leading figure among the grammarian-philosophers of his time who subscribed to one variety of the *sphota* theory. The doctrine of *sphota* in the grammarians' version argued that words are not merely a collection or sequence of phonemes. They are signs that help us identify meaning. However, meaning has a prephonetic existence, and thus meaning is at once identical with the sequence of phonemes and, at the same time, transcends the phonetic representation. *Sphota* is the term used by the grammarians, the *vaiyakaranas*, to denote meaning that exists in preverbal and, therefore, eternal form. Bhartrihari's concept of *kala* (time) was closely linked to his concept of *sphota*. In his thesis, they both appear fragmented in language, and are seemingly dependent on duration and sequence, but have in their essential form a nonfragmented and, therefore, eternal existence. Just as meaning in the human cognition has its source in *sphota*, time and tense in the human cognition have their origin in *kala*. And, again, just as *sphota* endows cognitive structures to material episodes of verbal articulation, *kala* endows cognitive structures to the temporal fragments perceived in the sequential events of human life. Clearly, then, time was completely analogous to meaning for Bhartrihari.

The mimansa view of meaning was that the phonetic sequence and structure of words have an absolute ontological status. Sequences of phonemes do indeed reveal the meaning of words, but the sequentiality by itself is no proof to say that meaning, or *sphota*, transcends or precedes the phonetic expression. Kumarila Bhatta maintained in his Slokavarttika that even if meaning is not entirely contingent as a linguistic category, there is no need to postulate an independent entity of *sphota* over and above the phonetic expression of meaning. In this thesis on cognition, as in Bhartrihari's, meaning is seen as being completely analogous to time. In fact, at the height of his polemics, Kumarila almost starts speaking of time instead of meaning. For instance, he writes, "The reaching of the preceding point of space becomes the cause of the reaching of the next point of space. . . . [Because] moments of the act of going succeed in bringing one to the desired space."

By the middle of the first millennium after Christ, Indian society had already acquired all its essential features. Powerful empires had been built, and the division of society between the cities and villages, its distribution among *varnas*, the rise of a coercive social and economic hierarchy had taken place, the *shastras* had been defined and given a sacred status, learning of these demarcated in caste and gender terms, and clan, lineage, and inheritance rules rooted in the minds of the people. Therefore, though new schools of thought kept emerging within the *ashrams* and *shalas*, the universities and the classrooms, they did not change the life and beliefs of the people as radically as the Upanishadic and Buddhist thought or the great epics had done in the past. So, even if the grammarians and the mimansa thinkers debated the nature of time, meaning, universe, and truth, the ancient doctrines continued to hold their sway, and when scholars and poets produced literary works, they allowed a generous intermixture of notions on these key cultural issues in their work. Kalidasa is probably the best known of the ancient Indian poets and dramatists. His *Abhignan Shakuntala* portrays the love between Prince Dushyanta and Shakuntala, who has been brought up as a hermitage girl gifted with divine beauty. Dushyanta happens to see Shakuntala while returning home from a war expedition, where he is invited to fight the demons and protect gods. He at once falls in love with her, and they marry secretly. He leaves her behind in the hermitage, promising to invite her to his capital. Shakuntala, lost in the thoughts of Dushyanta, forgets to entertain a visiting seer, who pronounces a curse on her, which would make Dushyanta forget her. Dushyanta indeed does forget her, and no longer able to bear her separation, Shakuntala, with his child growing in her womb, starts for the capital. On the way, while crossing a river, she loses the ring given to her by Dushyanta with which she could prove her identity. In his court, after being denied by him, she is not able to prove that she was indeed married to him. A divine intervention becomes necessary for the recovery of Dushyanta's memory and his recognition of Shakuntala as his lawful wife.

In Kalidasa's depiction of the story, as also in the response of the audience to the plot over the last seventeen centuries, Dushyanta has rarely been blamed for causing Shakuntala so much grief. His denial of Shakuntala as his wife has rarely been seen as an instance of denial of truth, but only a temporary lapse of memory. That truth shall prevail is taken for granted by the Indian mind brought up on the worldview presented in the Upanishads and the epics, and its temporary abnegation is not perceived as sin.

Probably the neglect of the scholarly views by the nonbrahmanical masses, or perhaps the emerging specter of invasion by other philosophical doctrines, led the eighth-century Shankara to revive the *shastras* and consolidate them into a system of metaphysical thought. At the heart of this system was the notion of the universe as created by an energy that is free from the laws of causation and time. Once again the substratum of existence as posited by the Upanishads was employed to define truth. Its only definition offered by Shankara was that it defied all definition. By this time metaphysical thought in India had come to be so inflexible that despite its logical rigor, it invited innumerable refutations arising out of the common wisdom of life. A new era in understanding truth was beginning to emerge in India.

From the beginning of the eleventh century, languages spoken by the masses in different regions of India started asserting themselves. The cultural forms that developed in classical India from the third to the tenth centuries started undergoing momentous changes at the beginning of the last millennium. The most fundamental of these was the emergence of new languages—*bhashas*—all over the Indian subcontinent. The new *bhashas* expressed regional and heterodox aspirations in protest against the hegemony of Sanskrit and the culture developed through that language, sanskriti. A similar movement occurred in the south with respect to Tamil, which, after a continuous history of two thousand years, branched into Telugu (eleventh century). Earlier, Kannada had already become an independent dialect of Tamil (fifth century). Nine hundred years later, Tamil and Kannada jointly gave birth to Malayalam (fourteenth century). In the north, the regional dialects known as Apabhramsa asserted themselves as independent languages. Consequently, the Middle Indo-Aryan dialect in the east split into Bangla and Oriya (tenth century). Subsequently, Bangla gave birth to Assamiya (thirteenth century). The northwestern dialect developed into Kashmiri (thirteenth century), Sindhi (fifteenth century), and Punjabi (fifteenth century). The western Apabhramsa of Middle Indo-Aryan distributed itself into Hindi (which until the beginning of the nineteenth century existed as several distinct dialects), Gujarati (eleventh century), and Marathi (eleventh century). The Hindi family of dialects developed autonomy in the fourteenth century. It also interacted with the Islamic languages—Persian, which was spoken in India from the thirteenth to the nineteenth centuries, and Arabic, in use from the eleventh to the nineteenth centuries—and produced a cantonment language, Urdu (thirteenth century), which later became a great literary language.

Interwoven with the rise of these modern Indian languages, the *bhashas*, is the story of the emergence of various religious sects. For about six centuries, from the eleventh to the sixteenth, India witnessed the miracle of a literary and philosophical creativity that produced a large number of saint-poets. Ranging from Basaveshwar in Kannada, Kabir and Mira in Central Indian dialects, Tukaram in Marathi, Narsi Mehta in Gujarati, and Nanak in Punjabi, to those minor poets who cultivated new forms of *bhajan*, *kirtan*, and heroic episodes or performative arts, these new saint-poets articulated for the masses a new, egalitarian philosophy of life. During the previous millennium, knowledge and learning were confined only to the brahmins and were taught in the *ashrams* and schools alone. Now they were brought close to the lives of those who produced, labored, tilled, and cultivated, those who were closely related to the material aspects of culture. Therefore, the new philosophy had a legitimate space for material aspects of life.

The saint-poets insisted that if brahman is present in everything, then everything is as sacred as brahman. Hence, the most trivial activity of life is as precious as the meditation of a *rishi* or the learning of a *shastri*. Therefore, it is not necessary to turn away from life in order to find the essence and meaning of life. This new philosophy acquired the name *bhakti*, devotion. The *bhakti* view of truth maintained that truth is a matter of conscience rather than that of consciousness. Bhakti was extremely weary of philosophical hairsplitting and mysticism negating life. It had an abundant reverence for the ordinary in the human realm. It maintained that all high values of life must be put in practice, that thought is meaningless if it is not reflected in action, and that all unity of persuasion and deed is indicative of truth.

It was during the *bhakti* period of Indian culture that for the first time the unity between brahman and dharma, between the Upanishadic ideal of contemplation and the Buddhist ideal of compassion, was emphasized as the goal of life. In doing this, *bhakti* internalized and personalized the idea of truth that the ancient scriptures had posited. The *bhakti* philosophers claimed that truth in order to be truth must be accompanied by *karuna*, compassion and love, and the one who had these qualities was the *satguru*, the teacher of truth, the true preceptor. The *bhakta*, the one in pursuit of truth, was urged to devote himself to the guru with all his soul and body. The body is palpably present in the *bhakti* view of the pursuit of truth, so much so that the devotion of the *bhakta* for his or her guru had very distinct erotic content. Thus, Mira, who made Krishna her guru, also thought of him as her consort. Clearly, then, *bhakti* was an energetic denial of the Upanishadic abstraction of truth as impersonal and undefinable. The energy of *bhakti* was so overpowering and it moved all classes of the society so radically in the direction of a theology without social discrimination that it gave rise to numerous regional but powerful movements that continue to thrive even today. These movements have come to be described by the term *sects*, though this term can barely represent the tremendous involvement of Indian masses in them.

There are three main manifestations of the irrational in the public domain in Indian culture: rituals, which have their source primarily in the Vedic practices; festivals, which are primarily linked to the seasons; and *yatras*, which perpetuate the philosophical and moral vision of the sects. The *yatras* are pilgrimages undertaken collectively by a vast number of persons to transact a relatively short distance. The *vari* to Pandharpur in Maharashtra or the Jagannath *yatras* all over India are the instances of *yatra* as a social phenomenon. Millions of Indians participate in them irrespective of their caste, gender, ethnic identity, and creed. These pilgrims form the particular sect. The pilgrimage is based on the belief that god, meaning, and truth can be discovered by each and every person by participation in the teaching of a saint, with a total *bhakti*. The central feature of the *bhakti* view of truth was that truth is yours if you are prepared to surrender yourself to it. This view survives in India as actively today as it did through the millennium of its emergence. The sects resulting from the *bhakti* movement have been the single most significant force liberating the Indian masses from the impersonal, nonmaterial, and abstract view of truth posited in ancient Indian thought and confined to Sanskrit alone. In that sense the *bhakti* movement was a fulfillment of the Buddhist ideal of surrender to truth as the aim of life, though of course the objects of devotion celebrated by the saint-poets were Rama and Krishna, drawn from the epics, and similarly the conceptual network within which the saints felt at home was rooted in the Upanishadic thought. The *bhakti* view of truth, therefore, accomplished a great philosophical synthesis and a social unity.

From the beginning of the sixteenth century, India started attracting European travelers and traders. The East India Company, which started its operations at the beginning of the seventeenth century, had established military supremacy in India by the middle of the eighteenth century. The British crown ruled India from 1858 to 1947. During this colonial period, it was but natural that the fields of knowledge established in India undergo a change. This change was radical. The most important of its features was that the written word came to occupy a far more important place in Indian culture than it had ever known before. Written contracts and written laws had become commonplace in India during the Islamic rules, particularly since paper as a material for writing became easily available during the thirteenth century. However, the question of livelihood had not been so rigidly tied down to the written word as it came to be connected during the colonial rule. During the Islamic rules, orality had not been made illegal. The colonial law privileged the written law over the oral contract beyond all proportions. Similarly, government jobs were available only to those who had received formal education in schools. Understandably, the difficulty of the colonial English rulers was linguistic. They required Indians with some knowledge of the English language to assist them in administration, and there had been no tradition of learning through oral memorization in the English language. Therefore, writing, and its technological manifestation in the form of printing, acquired a tremendous importance in the culture produced in India during the colonial period. The inevitable consequence of this shift was that truth came to be associated with its representation in written and printed form alone. In the law courts established in India by the colonial government, in order to have a legal validity, a testimony had to be preceded by the oath of truth. Besides, the oath of truth had to be declared by touching the copy of a written text such as the Bible, Koran, or Gita. Thus truth in its oral form had to have a sanction and legitimation from some written form of truth such as a scripture. Quite interestingly, most of the brahman class persons who belonged to the first generation of Indians to take to the colonial English education opted to be lawyers, in the process accepting this new definition of truth.

The colonial accent on truth as writing had an ominous implication for the oral tradition of those who could not write. It is necessary to differentiate the oral tradition of the scholars learning to recite the Vedas and other liturgical texts and the oral tradition of the *bhaktas* following the sects established after the medieval saints. The brahmans were always taught how to read and write. Their oral learning stemmed from the concern for the phonetic and musicological purity of the scriptures. The *bhaktas* as a class had little access to writing. When the British established modern schools and universities in India, the brahmans quickly fitted into the new mold; the *bhaktas* had difficulty in doing so, owing to their rural location and economic handicap. Therefore, while the new education brought with it the promise of a new social mobility, the caste structure soon acquired the characteristics of a class distinction, too. Truth as writing, and conversely, writing as truth had a significant role to play in the formation of the classes in nineteenth-century India. The process of liberation set in by *bhakti* thus received a reversal during the colonial period. It was not surprising, therefore, that the man who became the leading figure in India's liberation struggle made a lifelong attempt to put truth as the crucial weapon, together with nonviolence, in his teaching of self-rule. Mohandas Karamchand Gandhi, known as Mahatma, insisted that freedom would be meaningless if those who sought it did not fully internalize truth and nonviolence. That he put truth even before nonviolence is often overlooked. But it is significant that he called his biography his *Experiments with Truth* rather than with nonviolence. *Experiments with Truth* yields a fuller understanding of Gandhi's thought if it is read together with his *Hind Swaraj*, written before Gandhi launched his work in India.

The central argument in *Hind Swaraj* is that political freedom by itself is meaningless if those who seek it become a mere copy of the colonizers. In saying this, he at once changed the tone of the contemporary political discourse and premised that the fight for freedom is a universal phenomenon in which the fighter must learn to possess and control himself. This control over oneself, *swaraj*, is what in Gandhi's view made a person a *satyagrahi*. Thus "insistence on truth" is the ultimate way to freedom. In other words, Gandhi was saying that self-control is freedom to be won through the insistence on truth. When, therefore, he wrote *Experiments with Truth*, he set out to describe how he gained, though falteringly, control over his desire for the gratification of the senses, and how in doing this he molded himself to be an ideal *satyagrahi*. The autobiography is the most authentic chronicle of the life of one of the greatest leaders that the world has seen, but more importantly it is the chronicle of Gandhi's understanding of truth as freedom. Gandhi's influence on Indian society has been phenomenal. His idea of *satyagraha* was widely accepted by the common people during the years of the freedom struggle. But probably because the influence was so pervasive, no one after him has touched the hearts of the Indian people in the same way. Gandhi had millions of followers, but very few or no equals at all. Therefore, his idea of truth, very firmly rooted in nonviolence and freedom gained through self-discipline, soon after his death degenerated into a mere political weapon used for gratification of lust and power. *Satyagraha* came to mean in the post-Gandhi years a demonstration of political strength.

However, it is not in the field of politics but rather in the field of technological control of social impulses that Gandhi's thought has been denied and defeated. Although there are some political parties and groups that even now swear by Gandhi's ideals of truth and nonviolence, there are no significant voices that oppose the control over the human senses by material technology. The notion of self-rule beginning with the disciplining of the body by seeking freedom from the body's dependence on material comforts no more finds takers in India, except in esoteric groups that do so for theological merit. Truth as understood by Gandhi is now rejected in the social life of India.

Indian independence brought with it not only the state-controlled economy and massive developmental projects, not only the rapid urbanization and demographic shifts, not only the increased economic disparity and political jingoism, but also a technology of constructing a dream world. This technology was related to the cinema industry.

During the second half of the nineteenth century, written literature had gained immense popularity in India. Similarly, performances based on written works of dramatic compositions had been becoming popular. The national struggle for freedom had made photography an essential feature of the print medium. The influence of Western art had created some new life in the field of painting. All these fields together, literature, painting, music, drama, and photography, collectively gave birth to the Indian cinema industry, which became extremely influential in the years following independence. The hypnotic influence of cinema on the Indian masses was enhanced by the elements of music and song, which have perennially attracted the Indian mind.

In a country overburdened by a population explosion and made poorer in material wealth by a prolonged colonial exploitation, an escape from the drab and unsavory reality was most welcome. In the postindependence years, the celluloid reality started capturing the imagination of people in such a way that the idiom of real-life emotions was completely overpowered by the depiction of emotions in cinema. Though this is very difficult for a non-Indian to imagine, the Indian masses have come to a cultural stage where separations, deaths, unions, hatred, joy, love, and ecstasy cannot be enjoyed on their own terms without the inevitable mediation of a cinematic depiction of such emotions. This is true in the urban and the semiurban areas, but the rural areas, too, are fast moving in that direction. Television appeared in the drawing room of an average middle-class Indian in small towns in the 1980s. With it also appeared the tantalizing invitation to participate in the great feast of instant sensory gratification called globalization. The fantasies built by cinema as reality, and the fashion shows, advertisements, and the proliferation of icons of happiness, together have captured the Indian mind and instilled in it a new notion of truth. In this notion, truth has only a virtual relation with the phenomenal world. It is omniscient. It can be constructed any which way, but it must have the ability to dazzle. It likes to be seen and noticed, and allows instant engagement of the subject-consciousness. It is in no need of any search, *sadhana*, experiment, suffering, or contemplation on the part of the seeker. It is ever ready to serve, to beseech, to invade and seduce. It seeks out the seeker.

The virtual truth created by the tinsel world of imagery presented relentlessly through the electronic and photographic media is a singular triumph of iconography on the human imagination. It presents icons of perfection that the eye recognizes as true while the mind is fully aware that they are made up. Globalized India, glorying in its freedom, jubilant in its proliferation of celluloid dreams, has come to accept that the unreal can be, when made up, truth.

In its festivals, *yatras*, strifes, disasters, caste struggles, parliament, schools, bazaars, temples, villages, newspapers, and drawing rooms, India lives up to all these notions of truth gathered over the three millennia. Truth for an Indian is at once brahman, dharma, pain, *shabda*, art, *bhakti*, freedom, and illusion. It is but a notion as at best it can be.

WORK CITED

Vivekananda, Swami. (1947). *The Complete Works of Swami Vivekananda*, vol. viii, p. 100. Hollywood, CA: Vedanta Press.

ABOUT THE AUTHORS

ALI BENMAKHALOUF teaches philosophy at the University of Nice. He has published *Averroès* (Les Belles Lettres, Paris, 2000).

GANESH DEVY taught literature at the Maharaja Sayajirao University of Baroda before moving into the area of tribal languages and oral literature. He has initiated a cultural movement among the tribal communities of western India and has set up the Tribal Academy at Tejgadh for carrying out research in tribal culture. He is the author of the book *Of Many Heroes* (1998).

YANG GUO-RONG is a Professor of Chinese philosophy at East China Normal University, Shanghai. Professor Guo-rong is the author of *Rationality and Value*.

BERTRAND OGILVIE is Professor of Philosophy and Psychoanalysis, teaching at l'Université de Paris X-Nanterre. His most recent publication was *Par Dela Masculin et Feminin (à propos de Françoise Héritier, Masculin/ Féminin II). Dissoudre la hiérarchie* (Éditions Odile Jacob, Paris, 2002).

DOUGLAS PATTERSON is an Assistant Professor of Philosophy at Kansas State University. He is the author of numerous essays, including "Theories of Truth and Convention T" in *Dialectica* and "What is a Correspondence Theory of Truth?" in *Synthese*.

DEBORAH POSEL is a Professor of Sociology and Director of the Wits Institute for Social and Economic Research (WISER) at the University of Witwatersrand. Her most recent book, coedited with Graeme Simpson, is *Commissioning the Past: Understanding South Africa's Truth and Reconciliation Commission* (Wits University Press, Johannesburg, 2002).